# THE VIRGIN MARY'S REVOLUTION

### or

## Love, and do what you will

### Gonzalo T. Palacios

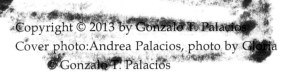

Printed in the United States of America

ISBN-13: 978-1482626865

ISBN-10:   1482626861

Sara Leeland Books
www.saraleelandbooks.net

# Dedicated to

Pope emeritus Benedict XVI, whose encyclical,
"God is Love," guided this book.

"Catholic Christendom is no simple exhibition
of religious absolutism, but it presents a continuous
picture of Authority and Private Judgment alternately
advancing and retreating as the ebb and flow
of the tide…"
--John Henry Newman

## Other books by Gonzalo T. Palacios

Desde Watergate hasta Chávez: diplomáticos, espías y farsantes en la capital del Imperio, Caracas, 2008 (banned in Venezuela).

From Watergate to Hugo Chavez, An ex-diplomat's memoirs, 2009.

VENEZUELA XXI, La Revolución de la Estupidez, Bogotá, 2011.

# THE VIRGIN MARY'S REVOLUTION

## CONTENTS

# PROLOGUE

The time has come when some memories of my life demand lives of their own. For the last 75 years, my mind has recorded a myriad of experiences, pleasant or painful, edifying or debasing, divine or profane. Initially, I was surprised; then somewhat amazed; and recently, simply delighted that each of those experiences revealed what I am all about.

The more I dwell on events that happened even seven decades ago (for instance, the death of my father), the clearer it is to me "that Love was a great god," as Socrates put it. During adolescence, testosterone obfuscated what Saint John of the Cross called "the science of love... an infused and loving knowledge of God, which enlightens the soul and enkindles it with love...." Even today I cannot claim "the state of perfection which consists in the perfect love of God," yet still I feel compelled to share what has been revealed to me in my life experiences.

We spend our entire lives asking: "who do you I am?" The following say pages suggest that the Virgin Mary's unconventional reply to her Divine Lover reveals both God's and our own identities.

Mary's *Fiat* taught us we were made by Love to love and to be loved. She deliberately rejected Mosaic Law and, in Pope Benedict's words, restored "a unity which creates love, a unity in which both God and man remain themselves and yet become fully one" (*Deus Caritas Est*, I, 10).

The Virgin Mary had launched the New Covenant; her Son sealed it with His blood. Yet, to this day, her friends, her Son's brothers and sisters, adhere to the old ways. Even the Church has refused to follow Mary's command, "do whatever He tells you." Instead of executing Jesus' Law, i.e. the Law of Love, our Father, we remain slaves of the Old, thus losing "the intrinsic link between that Love and the reality of human love."

> --Gonzalo T. Palacios
> Kensington, MD
> Feast of the Annunciation, 2013

# INTRODUCTION

The immediate response to Jesus Christ and to his New Covenant was to reject both of them. Even his followers were divided in their interpretation of Jesus' message. A few of them identified totally with their "Lord and Master." Others adhered to the Laws of Moses, but accepted Jesus as their long-awaited Messiah.

This disagreement threatened to break up the nascent Church. The Virgin Mary's Mystical Son, the Church, seemed in danger of being aborted: "...after the discussion had gone on a long time, Peter stood up and addressed them. 'It would only provoke God's anger now, surely, if you imposed on the disciples the very burden that neither we nor our ancestors were strong enough to support? Remember, we believe we are saved in the same way as they are: through the grace of the Lord Jesus.' This silenced the entire assembly...." (Acts, 15, 5-12).

That first Council of the Church (Jerusalem, 50 AD) ended the discussion, but the disparate viewpoints persisted. Those members of the Church most closely associated with the powerful of the Earth continued to use Mosaic Laws to control humanity.

More than an act of rebellion, the Virgin Mary's

utter rejection of her Jewish heritage and of Moses' Covenant was the initial salvo of the revolution that restored us to our original status of sons of God. The Virgin Mary's tryst with her Divine Lover provided us the Messiah, the Liberator who freed us from sin but not from the oppression of Caesar. The execution of Jesus was the ultimate expression of His Love.

After Golgotha, humanity was free to love and to be in Love eternally. But to be truly free of the rules, laws, and traditions that defined our sins, Love demands we do His bidding: our total commitment, without attachments of any sort, not even to one's earthly life.

Roman satraps and power-sharing Jewish collaborators executed a man suspected of exerting a new sort of power, the power to Love. The Virgin Mary, freed from the Old Covenant laws and cultural restrictions, gave birth to the New in the person of her son Jesus.

We were no longer slaves to Caesar or to the flesh; we were restored to our place in God's "Kingdom." We were free to Love, as St. Augustine wrote in his Seventh Homily on Saint John: "Love, and do what you will."

Those in power still adhere to the Mosaic Laws and use them to control us. Every time we preach Jesus' good news, "all Hell breaks lose." Immediately the Grand Inquisitors expel our liberator, our Messiah, and his followers from "their" community: "for nothing has ever been more insupportable for a man and a human society than freedom" (Fyodor Dostoyevsky, *The Brothers Karamazov*).

History shows that those in control always do whatever is necessary to retain power, at the expense of their authority. In an effort to avoid a confrontation with our own "grand inquisitors." Throughout this book, the word 'myth' is equivalent to 'story,' as one that describes a mystery. This book, *The Virgin Mary's Revolution*, uses sources whose orthodoxy is beyond question, such as St. Augustine, papal encyclicals and directives, documents from the Second Vatican Council, and the Catechism of the Catholic Church. Most of Part I leads to the event that triggered the "Revolution" (Chapters 10 and 11). Chapter 1, "The Evil of Rumors," points to an absence of love in relation to our fellow human beings. Chapter 2 takes a fleeting glance at our evolutionary biological system and asks, "Who is authorized to frustrate the system?" Finally, Chapters 3 and 4 describe contemporary scientific information that influences our understanding of human sexuality.

The remaining pages constitute a request that we return to Jesus' authority, the New Covenant of Love. To do so we must abandon further adherence to invalid laws and traditions, for it borders on idolatry.

That is what the Virgin Mary did.

# PART I

# LOVE AND FREEDOM

Part I of *The Virgin Mary's Revolution* describes the interconnection that exists between Love and freedom. Transcending its temporal condition, human intelligence leads to the eternal Present. Existential experiences of the transcendent involve the illumination of faith and the use of myths to express them. The Virgin Mary's pregnancy was one such experience.

## CHAPTER 1

# THE EVIL OF RUMORS

The abdominal surgery had left me weaker than I had expected; fortunately, two weeks later I was recovering quite well. In fact, by the end of the month my gastroenterologist allowed me to drive and soon I was back in the classroom. I teach Philosophy and Philosophy of Religion, both of which engage important contemporary ethical issues of our society. Issues related to the evil of rumors and the rumors of evil frequently come up in class—and in the rest of my life.

I had been home from the hospital about a week when my wife informed me I had received an email from a life-long friend I'd first met as a freshman in high school. Thinking that it was a "Get Well" message I asked her to read it to me. "Better not," she said, knowing of my resolve not to read or argue politics or religion with anyone, much less with my friends. Many years ago I had promised myself not to jeopardize old friendships trying to explain why I did not share their points of view.  I stopped joining all conversations about political or religious ideologies.

My wife did tell me that the last three lines declared that Ms. "B" was a lesbian (I have substituted letters for names to avoid a rumor). Later that day, I saw the "Subject" heading still in my laptop: "Why "B" can't relate." My friend had forwarded the demeaning rumor to numerous acquaintances and relatives. I have edited the message in order to lessen its deleterious effect: in part, it read as follows:        "Apr 19 (2012), Cheers.

> In case you have been on a different planet, Hilary is the lobbyist, pundit, and Obama supporter who made the statement that Ann, a stay-at-home mother, "has actually never worked a day in her life." In addition to their vastly different political viewpoints, the following item from Hilary's Wikipedia biography may explain why she *dissed* Ann. ...Hilary is a lesbian.... She and her ex-husband separated in 2006.   No word on what happened to the kids..."

True or not, the last statement is obviously intended to malign Hilary's character. Ironically, such an intention presupposes a traditional Judeo-Christian understanding of human sexuality. That moral view, along with other human values, have literally constituted our America, differentiating this country from all other nations in the history of humanity.

Equality, freedom, and justice, *endowed by their Creator* (*the separate and equal station to which the Laws of Nature and of Nature's God entitle them*), guided our legal system and gave citizens of the United States the possibility of living in a peaceful and harmonious society. Respect for one another's life is protected by our judiciary, whose authority is, to this day, directly derived from our belief in our Creator, specifically, the Judeo-Christian God.

American culture today is squandering the strengths that characterize America for most of us: respect, decency, freedom, tolerance, truthfulness, justice, and compassion. We are wasting these virtues inherited from the Judeo-Christian and Greco-Roman cultures. We are losing America not because *they* are invading our country — regardless of their ethnicity, foreigners are not taking over our country. Nor can religious groups, not even atheists, be held responsible for the loss of our values and beliefs. Our economic system has deteriorated to the point that it not longer serves our democratic system of government, but that is no reason for losing America's fundamental values.

Instead, we have fallen into a trap set by our own quest for Power and by our Greed, a trap called "class warfare."

Personal attacks against "Everyman" are a daily occurrence. Intolerance and aggression are now considered proper courses of action to achieve whatever goal is sought (win at any cost is the only rule). Slanders and rumors propagated by political ideologues and by insecure individuals partially explain the destruction of our value-system. Such social behavior was not accepted in our America only a generation ago.

The following story from Jewish folklore illustrates why we are losing America. It tells us about a person who spread a rumor concerning his neighbor. Soon, the whole community had heard the rumor. Later, he learned that the rumor was untrue. The person was very sorry and went to a wise elder of the community to seek advice; he wanted to repair the damage he had inflicted on his neighbor.

The elder told the man, "Go to your home and take a feather pillow outside. Rip it open and scatter the feathers, then return to me tomorrow."

The man did as the elder had instructed. The next day, he visited the elder. The elder said, "Now, go and collect the feathers you scattered yesterday and bring them back to me." The person went home and searched for the feathers, but the wind had carried them all away. The sad man returned to the elder and said, "I could find none of the feathers I scattered yesterday."

"You see," said the elder, "it's easy to scatter the feathers but impossible to get them back." So it is with rumors; it doesn't take much to spread hurtful words, but once you do, you can never completely undo the damage."[1]

These days, the feathers of the torn pillow represent e-mails, tweet messages, and radio and television comments.[2] For the sake of restoring decency, love, union, freedom and justice to our country, we need to *stop participating in rumors of any kind.* Scandal (rumor) is a word or action *evil* in itself, which occasions another's spiritual ruin[3].

## CHAPTER 2

# ABOUT LIFE

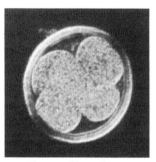

**Four cell embryos**

What comes first, the chicken or the egg; a human *being*, or a human *becoming* process? Maybe the question should be: what is more important and necessary, a human's being or a human's becoming process?

Let me explain. A being is what anything is: it is not what something was or will be, but that which it always is, from the beginning to the end of its life. A being sustains its own becoming; that is to say, its own life process. We know that for all live beings, life is the passage from what it was to what it is, now. It is also the passage to what it will be from what it is, now. A being is continuously present during its own process of becoming, otherwise there would be nothing to become. The process of becoming is not identical to the being that is present to it, just as human life is not identical to the one who lives it. But the being of anything – whatever it is – contains and sustains its entire becoming process.

Have you ever grown a plant from its seed? As a child, I remember science classes in which the teacher would have us grow different plants in a glass container filled with black dirt. We would place the seed against the glass and in a matter of days we could see it becoming a plant. After breaking apart, the seed took the shape of white thin roots and some days later, one shoot would seek the surface and the light and air from above. Once out in the warmth of the sun, the vertical shoot would produce two tiny leaves, then four, and so on as it became the plant contained in the original seed.

Some of my classmates' seeds had no life in them. Other children, each for his own reason, would empty the dirt from the glass container and stop the growth of the plant. These were the same guys who enjoyed pulling off flies' wings or feeding live goldfishes to their cats. Our science teacher gave them a failing grade for deliberately frustrating the natural growth of a being.

Similarly, a human's *being* is present at the beginning of its own process of *becoming*, otherwise nothing would evolve. Like the seeds in my science classes, a fertilized human egg begins to develop only if it has that which sustains life, to wit, a human's being, a soul. *Only if a human being is present – not just the fertilized egg – does human life begin.* That individual human being *sustains his or her life* for its duration.

Just as the life of a plant consists in continuous changes that begin with the disintegration of its seed, a human's existence begins when a new being, a human being, animates (*anima* in Latin means 'soul') the fertilized ovum. It is at this point that the continuous changes we call "a human life" begin. Those changes will go on for as long as the human's being is present *to* them.

As soon as humans appeared on Earth, questions and doubts began. Other forms of life do not question or doubt; they obey the laws of their beings, the natural law. What Aristotle called the animal or the vegetative soul, begins and sustains the becoming process of each living plant or animal.[4]

The human process of becoming – "life" – differs from all others in that our souls endow it with the specific "power of thinking."[5] The power of thinking is the power to question and to doubt. In fact, that power enables us to reject or to accept our own questions and our own doubts: "There is nothing in me that I cannot question." [6]

Thinking enables us to raise questions: "This element of doubt is a condition of all spiritual life."[7] Becoming a human being will always include questioning and doubting; "Doubt is the necessary tool of knowledge," as theologian Paul Tillich has said.

At all times, in our century or in Cain and Abel's time, humans by nature ask questions. Questions like: "Am I my brother's keeper?" Do I have the right and perhaps the obligation to terminate my own or another person's life? Does every new human being have a right to his own process of becoming, to his own life? It is important to illustrate this last point with St. Thomas Aquinas' words:

> "… the child's *soul*… is distinct from the *soul* of the mother because the body of the animated infant is already formed, and consequently distinct from the body of the mother." [8]

Does anyone or any institution have the *authority* (not the power) to end someone's life? Does the validity of the following words depend on social agreement?

"We hold these truths to be self-evident, that all men are created equal, that they are endowed by their Creator with certain unalienable rights that among, these are Life, Liberty and the pursuit of Happiness"?

In other words, does my soul, my being, have the *unalienable* right to animate my body from its beginning until its end? As some of my friends failed to grow plants in our science class in school, will I fail because I can frustrate the natural growth of the life within myself? If so, will I flunk my life course?

## CHAPTER 3

# MY GENERATION'S
# SEXUAL REVOLUTION

"The generation which commences a revolution rarely completes it."   --Thomas Jefferson to John Adams, 1823.

In 1953 some of my high school classmates (Archmere, Claymont, DE, '55) were certain that the sexual revolution had begun. Many of us were naïve enough to believe we had contributed to its beginning.

Given the fact that we had entered that period of life called "adolescence," our brains were no longer being irrigated by oxygenated blood alone. Sexual revolution, indeed! Rather than a revolution, it was Darwinian evolution following its inexorable path in each one of us. Our production of testosterone had increased tenfold, thereby accelerating our sexual development. Among young men, the gradual awareness of their rationality, its function, and its *modus operandi*, enables them to learn from a plethora of new experiences. But while we were learning to reason, we were also under the influence, if not the control of, testosterone. Our intellectual growth intermingled with that of our sexuality, constantly confronting our spiritual activities with our physiological reactions.

It was the right time for our English Lit teachers to introduce us to Dickens' *Tale of Two Cities*:

> "It was the best of times, it was the worst of times, it was the age of wisdom, it was the age of foolishness, it was the epoch of belief, it was the epoch of incredulity, it was the season of Light, it was the season of Darkness, it was the spring of hope, it was the winter of despair, we had everything before us, we had nothing before us, we were all going direct to Heaven, we were all going directly the other way–in short, *the period was so far like the present period,* that some of its noisiest authorities insisted on its being received, for good or for evil, in the superlative degree of comparison only."

Testosterone in our brains also created an intellectual milieu in which rationality and egoism were confused. We tended to accept unquestioningly Ayn Rand's simplistic ideology, a concoction of Nietzsche's slave-master morality and Mill's utilitarian pleasure-pain ethics. Who but an immature, self-centered teenager would be willing to believe that:

> "...every human being is an end in himself [...] man must live for his own sake, neither sacrificing himself to others nor sacrificing others to himself. To live for his own sake means that *the achievement of his own happiness is man's highest moral purpose*." [9]

College prep schools frequently become petri dishes for a narcissistic culture, such as we have in the United States. One bright October morning, two months before the first issue of *Playboy* magazine appeared on the stands of drugstores, Father Joseph Kelly decided to inspect our rooms. The inside of my locker was covered with magazine photographs of Marilyn Monroe and Grace Kelly.

"You're grounded this week-end, Gonzalo," the Norbertine friar said. No explanation was needed: Father Kelly did not even have to order me to clean-up my locker. Testosterone made me do it, I thought.

## CHAPTER 4

# THE PILL

In a 1960 press conference, President Eisenhower declared that birth control "is not a proper political or government activity, function, or responsibility." That same year Margaret Sanger and Katherine McCormick suggested that an oral contraceptive should be made available to women.

In direct contradiction to the President's views, that year the FDA approved G. D. Searle's petition to produce and market The Pill. By the end of December, Searle's company had made over $37 million in sales of The Pill. Many women were convinced that finally the sexual revolution had begun.[10] This was also the decade of Friedan's *The Feminine Mystique* (1963) and Ayn Rand's *The Virtue of Selfishness* (1961). Men were threatened by the new power given to women by male researchers Gregory Pincus, John Rock, Frank Colton, Carl Djerassi, and others.

On 7 September 1968, a "Freedom Trash Can" was placed on the Atlantic City Boardwalk and filled with high-heeled shoes, false eyelashes, curlers, hairspray, makeup, *Vogue* and *Playboy* magazines, corsets, girdles, and bras. That was the extent of my generation's sexual revolution. The *Playboy* "philosophy" and other symbols of female submission ended up in an Atlantic City trash can, incapable of convincing American women that they had revolutionized human sexuality and overtaken their male oppressors.[11]

The bra burners were no match for sexual counterrevolutionaries like the brassiere manufacturers and the incipient transplant industry. In 1962 male researchers Frank Gerow and Thomas Cronin fabricated the first silicone breast implant and Timmie Jean Lindsey became the first woman to receive the new sexual enhancer.

Jefferson's prognostication about incomplete revolutions was vindicated once again: "The generation which commences a revolution rarely completes it." That is because few people know what constitutes a true revolution.

Ironically, another woman would write the most intelligent analysis on the subject, *On Revolution* (1963). In her essay Hannah Arendt explained the misunderstanding of that socio-political phenomenon: "Both liberal democrats and Marxists have misunderstood the drama of modern revolutions," she wrote, "because they have not understood what was actually revolutionary about these revolutions"

Arendt then explains why there has been no sexual revolution in our time:

> "The outbreak of most revolutions has surprised the revolutionist groups and parties no less than all others, and there exists hardly a revolution whose outbreak could be blamed upon their activities."[12]

Ignorance of what a true revolution is and of the real nature of human sexuality are constant elements of our culture. In 2008, a leading magazine announced "The New Sexual Revolution" with a cover photograph of a man's hand holding a blue, rhomboid-shaped pill labeled "VGR 50."

Once again, 'Love' was defined in terms of sexual activities produced and controlled chemically. And, as in earlier years, this "new sexual revolution" was measured in terms of sales and profits:

> "That could explain why U. S. sales of the little blue pill and two newer drugs have skyrocketed to more than $1.5 billion a year…."[13]

Our human desire to control our own individual evolution, or that of the Universe, blinds us to the obvious: Evolution transforms matter in time and space; *revolution transforms evolution by transcending it in the Present*. Because it is coming into being, becoming does not begin or sustain itself: *nemo dat quod non habet.*

Some humans experience an authentic epistemological and ethical revolution when they first learn that the entire time/space continuum [Creation] is made, sustained, and contained in the Present. From its very genesis, Evolution—the time/space continuum—is nothing but an expression of the Present.

As Tennyson wrote:

"Let there be light and there was light: 'tis so:
For was, and is, and will be, are but is;
*And all creation is one act at once,*
The birth of light: but we that are not all,
As parts, can see but parts, now this, now that,
And live, perforce, from thought to thought,
  and make
One act a phantom of succession: Thus
Our weakness somehow shapes the shadow,
  Time;
But in the shadow will we work, and mould
The woman to the fuller day.'"

(Tennyson, *The Princess*, III).

Our senses and our brains operate in time and space. Information about the Present is never *in* the Present; like television bleeps, there is a time delay between our senses, the processed perception, and its expression. But the Present does reveal itself in the Past (historical facts, memories) and in the Future (precognition, imagination, intuition, prediction).

All of time and space is *in the eternally inscrutable Present* or it is not at all.

> "Then came, at a predetermined moment,
> A moment in time and out of time,
> A moment not out of time, but in time, in what
> We call history..."
>
> (T.S. Eliot, *The Rock)*

These revelations from the mysterious Present produce substantial re-definitions. It is human intelligence that endows the revelations with meaning. Man and Cosmos, for example, are no longer merely temporal phenomena; both partake of the eternal Present.

CHAPTER 5

# SEXUALITY AND RELIGIONS

Throughout the history of humanity many institutions and religions have spread mistaken and detrimental concepts about our sexuality. There have been as many reasons for this phenomenon as there have been such institutions and religions in the world. The family unit is the most important conduit of human sexual customs; religions are a close second. One develops sexually and learns sexual behavior relative to one's family and one's religion or lack thereof.

Parents, elders, religious leaders, and governments are more often than not motivated by power. From time immemorial, power, not authority, energizes the individual's sexual development. It behooves us to analyze the connection between these authorities and other institutions that inform us about our sexuality.

The concept of power is as different from that of authority as sexual morality differs from sexual ethics. The temporal and material nature of power and of sexual morality makes them similar to each other.

The perennial and immaterial nature of authority and of ethics defines these two. All temporal powers oppress and eventually destroy whatever and whomever they control. All legitimate authority creates and liberates its creatures. Sexual ethics builds character, but temporal social customs define sexual *morality*. Sexual mores derive their power from the fears that exist in their societies:

> "In Australia the regular penalty for sexual intercourse with a person of a forbidden clan is death.... Even in casual amours the clan prohibitions are strictly observed; any violations of these prohibitions are regarded with the utmost abhorrence and are punished by death."[14]

Sexual fears pass from generation to generation. Sexual fears have inspired artists, philosophers, and religious leaders through the ages. For example, Aeschylus' creations expressed the fear of incestous and violent sex: "The death of honor, rolled in dust and blood, /Slain for a woman's sin, a false wife's shame!"[15] Another myth, "The Rape of Europa," presents us with the consequences of violent sex.

Epicurus and, centuries later, Jeremy Bentham and John Stuart Mill, reduced human happiness to mere pleasure or the absence of pain. Human sexuality would then be no more than animal satisfaction.

In the Renaissance, Giovanni Boccaccio, wrote about how sexual flippancy erodes social ethics, as in the following necrophilic passage of his *Decameron (Novel IV):*

> "Twas night while he thus mused; and forthwith, observing strict secrecy in his departure, he got him to horse with a single servant, and halted not until he was come to the place where the lady was interred; and having opened the tomb he cautiously entered it. Then, having lain down beside her, he set his face against hers; and again and again, weeping profusely the while, he kissed it.
>
> Obeying which impulse, he laid his hand her bosom, and keeping it there some time, felt, as he thought, her heart faintly beating. Whereupon, banishing all fear, and examining the body with closer attention, he discovered that life was not extinct, though he judged it but scant and flickering: and so, aided by his servant, he bore her, as gently as he might, out of the tomb, set her before him upon his horse, and brought her privily to his house at Bologna"

Shakespeare described the fatal consequences of incest in *Hamlet,* a tragedy in which all the protagonists die. Friedrich Nietzsche misrepresented the message of Jesus: "The church fights passion with excision in every sense: its practice, its 'cure', is *castration*…. It has at all times laid the stress of discipline on extirpation (of sensuality…). But an attack on the roots of passion means an attack on the roots of life: the practice of the church is *hostile to life*."[16]

Nietzsche chose to ignore Jesus' message regarding the passion of love: "A man can have no greater love than to lay down his life for his friends" (*John* 15; 13). In the Twentieth Century artists like Pablo Picasso, Gabriel Garcia Marquez, Pablo Neruda, and countless others often described human sexuality as a means of oppression.

The folklore that has grown from and around human sexuality includes all sorts of fantasies, myths, and outright falsehoods. A culture of sexual power has produced power concepts such as patriarchies, matriarchies, children's "legitimacy," gender injustice, and religious rituals.

When the people of Israel settled in the Promised Land and became the depositories of the Mosaic Law, they were tempted to place their safety and their happiness in something other than the Word of the Lord, to wit, in material goods and power. These other 'divinities' are, in fact, empty and futile idols. The Mosaic Law remained, but after the Annunciation, Mary relegated it to the dustbin of history. As Pope Benedict XVI warned in September 2012:

> "This is a serious risk in every religion, one which Jesus encountered in His own time, and unfortunately it can also arise in Christianity. Thus Jesus' words...against the Scribes and Pharisees must make us think. Jesus repeats the words of Isaiah: 'This people honor me with their lips, but their hearts are far from me; in vain do they worship me, teaching human precepts as doctrine'. ... In his Letter, the Apostle James also warns against the danger of false religiosity", the Holy Father concluded."[17]

CHAPTER 6

# THE ETERNAL PRESENT

Our thinking process enables us to see through time and space. Our intelligence redefines us as "be-ings-in-*eternity*." Our life span takes on an entirely different significance; human intelligence tran-scends the limitations of the cosmic "stuff" that con-stitutes us. As long as man is in the process of be-coming, his intelligence benefits from the sort of enlightenment described by men like the Buddha, Mohammed, Zoroaster, and Jesus. This transcen-dental "light" is commonly called "faith." Faith en-ables us to understand the *supernatural* experience of being-in-the Present.

The Present, then, is that which *is* and not that which was or will be. The Present is a foundational mystery which lies beyond our comprehension. We understand not what *is*, but what *was* perceived by our senses: "Nothing is in the intellect that was not first in the senses."[18] Is the energy that produces the movement from ignorance to knowledge the same energy that moves us from indifference to loving?

What is the Energy-cause that begins and can alter the evolutionary process? Questions will always remain. In a manner analogous to other creation myths, the story that the "Big Bang" generated the Cosmos cannot be ascertained using scientific epistemology.

The Alpha moment of C o s m i c Evolution— the "Big Bang' instant or t h a t of human life— cannot be established by scientific experimentation anymore than its Omega point. Intelligent explanations of the Alpha and the Omega of the Cosmos and of each individual human life transcend sensorial information.

Whether we comprehend it or not, transcending one's own intelligence requires *faith*. As St. Anselm of Canterbury wrote, faith seeks understanding:

> "If anyone does not know, either because he has not heard or because he does not believe, that there is one nature, supreme among all existing things, who alone is self-sufficient in his eternal happiness, who through his omnipotent goodness grants and brings it about that all other things exist or have any sort of well-being, and a great many other things that we must believe about God or his creation, *I think he could at*

*least convince himself of most of these things by reason alone, if he is even moderately intelligent."* (M1)

The following three requirements are basic for an authentic revolution to occur:

1. A true revolution *transforms* temporal reality;
2. A true revolution *expresses* Reality in "no time;"
3. A true revolution re-defines realities perceived in time and space.

With these ideas, it is now possible to understand how the Annunciation sparked the Virgin Mary's revolution: a true revolution of human sexuality began with her consent to her Lover.

CHAPTER 7

# "Love is the Energy of Creation"[19]

*Venus von Willendorf*,
**24,000–22,000 BCE**

What do Plato, Dante, Jehovah's Witnesses, Dorothy L. Sayers, and Pope Benedict XVI have in common? Why is it that seldom, if ever, one finds objections to Dante's concluding affirmation in his *Divine Comedy* that "love moves the sun and the other stars?" Or to Eryximachos assertion in Plato's *Symposium* that "Love as a whole has great and mighty power, or rather in a word, omnipotence"?

Jehovah's Witnesses claim that the Holy Spirit is God's "energy," Dorothy L. Sayers identifies Love as the energy of all creations, and Pope Benedict XVI frequently synthesizes these insights in most of his writings and lectures. Throughout his first encyclical, *Deus Caritas Est*, the Pope refers to "God's creative love," and in a 1981 Lenten homily in Munich he restates "that there is only one power everywhere...this same power – which created the earth and the stars and which bears the whole universe...."

Benedict XVI reiterates the omnipotence and omnipresence of God's creative love in the second homily of the series: "...God created the universe in order to enter into a history of love with humankind. He created it so that love could exist."

To summarize: from the earliest of times to the present, human beings have believed or taken for granted that there is a creative force or energy that transcends Evolution. Love, the omnipotent, the omni-present creative Energy of the Universe reveals itself in the time/space continuum. The Supernatural Energy of Creative Love generates Nature's Evolution. Love is present in all acts of creation. In other words, Love is *omnipresent* and *eternal* (ever Present). The experience of Love divinizes our temporal existence. To partake of Love's creative act, that is to say, to conjugate the Verb Love, is fundamental for human perfection. Human happiness involves attaining human perfection, the ultimate reason for our creation. Faith in the Present ("the Alpha and Omega") enlightens human intelligence, enabling it to understand that its Creator, its creative Energy, and its Creation are three different manifestations of one and the same Author.[20]

**Pietá, by Michelangelo**

The transubstantiation of a block of marble (or bread and wine) into something other than itself does not happen by chance; it is not a phase of the evolutionary process. Neither the physical mass of the artist nor that of the marble has the power to bring about this transformation. It is the spiritual force of the artist's being that energizes the potentiality of the marble to become a new entity, the sculpture, or the Body of Christ. Operating in the perennial Present and enlightened by it, our intelligence makes it possible for us to communicate spiritually with the artistic creators of the past.

How long was the *Pietà* potentially in Michelangelo's 20 year-old heart before it was "delivered" into time and space? He may not have been aware of its existence until his hands shaped the magnificent sculpture. We do know he made a careful selection in Carrara— nothing but the purest white marble would be good enough for his figures.[21]

Inexplicably, the young sculptor "witnessed" the events at Golgotha circa 35 A.D. His depiction of the young mother with her dead son in her lap over fourteen centuries later is timeless. The *Pietà* partakes in "the eternal and divine" about which Aristotle taught his students when speaking of biological reproduction:

> "...the most natural act is the production of another like itself, an animal producing an animal, a plant a plant, in order that, as far as its nature allows, *it may partake in the eternal and divine*. That is the goal towards which all things strive..."[22]

To this day, Michelangelo Buonarroti is Present to us: his creative spirit perpetually animates his creations.

Those of us willing to transcend sense perceptions, be they seeing, hearing, touching, smelling, or tasting, can experience the beauty and truth that lie under (in Latin, *sub-stans*, "under-standing") paintings, music or poetry, architecture, sculptures, or bodies, even a good wine or a refreshing sip of pure water.

Whether we face the works of Velázquez or Picasso, of Beethoven or Brubeck, of Virgil or Dante, of John C. Portman or Charles-Édouard Jeanneret (Le Corbusier), of Alexandros of Antioch (Venus of Milo), or of the Benedictine Monks whose spirits live in their champagne, the creative energy of true artists transcend time and space: they are always Present.

All artists, human or divine, re-present and re-produce Love in their works, again and again... as long as the material medium employed survives.

## CHAPTER 8

# Motion, Life, and Sexuality

**Copernicus,** *De Revolutionibus*
*orbium coelestium.*

Darwinian evolution developed human sexuality. Its primary function was to reproduce the life of human animals and to assure the survival of their genes. Eventually, evolution produced *complementary bi-sexuality* as a different means of biological reproduction among a variety of creatures, including human beings.

After millions of years of evolution the nature of human sexuality experienced a true revolution[23]; it would be *substantially* transformed. This *revolution* of the evolution of human biology redefined the very essence of human sexuality, its functions, and its manifestations. From then on, human sexuality was no longer a time / space phenomenon: it became a revelation of eternal Life, a self-sustaining motion. This one and only sexual revolution would alter us substantially, *if we choose to be part of it.*

### Perpetual Motion

"One of the most intriguing facets of quantum mechanics — to scientists and science fiction fans alike — is that of persistent current: a natural electric current that flows *perpetually without a power source,*" writes John Urwin.[24]

Urwin goes on to explain the recent experiments in the field of quantum currents conducted by Yale Professors Jack Harris and Leonid Glazman. The title and the opening paragraph makes us aware that the article will not necessarily be understood; its intended readers include both scientists well versed in the ideas of quantum mechanics and those of us who may consider it science fiction.

Although *perpetual motion* is not properly defined, Urwin concludes optimistically: "Besides putting to rest a decades old debate, these elegant experiments once again confirm the accuracy of quantum mechanics and reveal the *strange* and *quirky beauty* of our universe."

Actually, Mr. Urwin's wishful thinking does not meet the standards of his mentors' elegant experiments. It is not the accuracy of quantum mechanics or the measurements of a hypothetical perpetual motion that reveals the beauty of our universe: it is the specifically human ability to read meaning into the hypotheses of quantum mechanics or the elegance of our measurements. Our intelligence enables us to see beauty—real, not fictional—in all creations.

### Perpetual Life

"The soldiers come out of the forest, carrying Jones' limp body. There is a little reddish-purple hole under his left breast. He is dead.

Smithers: 'Well, they did for yer right enough, Jonesy, me lad! Dead as a 'erring!"

(Eugene O'Neill's *The Emperor Jones,* last scene.)

Half a century later, Hannah Arendt also wrote about being "Dead as a 'erring!", but not in cinematomatographic terms: "Without the breath of life the human body is a corpse; without thinking the human mind is dead. This is...the metaphor that

Aristotle tried out: 'The activity of thinking [*energeia*] is life.'"[25]

Arendt then explains how the inherent law of the thinking activity can be tolerated only by a god; it applies to a human being only "now and then, during which time he is godlike; he is '*unceasing motion, which is motion in a circle.*"[26]

Thinking, then, reveals the characteristics of perpetual or "unceasing motion", which, according to Aristotle, St. Basil, St. Augustine, and others, reflect man's god-like nature:

> "The mind is a wonderful thing, and therein
> we possess that which is after the image of
> the Creator. And the operation of the mind
> is wonderful… in its *perpetual motion*…"[27]

As St. Augustine put it: "Man then is not an image as the Only-begotten Son is, but made after a sort of image and likeness."[28]

John Urwin is correct in placing the debate about perpetual motion in the past. He errs when he states that the issue is "decades old," since the search for a source of perpetual motion goes back at least to the Age of Reason or the Scientific Revolution, to thinkers like Nicholas Copernicus (1473-1543), Blaise Pascal (1623-1662), and Jean-Jacques Rousseau (1712-1778).

If human motion is human life, perpetual human motion is perpetual human life. Creation is in perpetual motion since it came into existence; humans are in perpetual motion once they are created.

Both natural phenomena and human experiences have causes not found in the course of cosmic evolution since it began some 14 billion years ago. This affirmation presupposes the existence of a concatenation of occurrences in Creation. Concatenated events cannot be attributed to anything or anyone *previous* to it: there is no "before" the first event, i.e., the creation of time and space. No time and no space, i.e., no Creation, means no motion, since all motion requires a 'here" and a "there" and a "now" and a "then."

### The Motion of Love and Human Sexuality

Thinking, we saw earlier, is one human activity which manifests our divine-like nature. Thinking best expresses how we are drawn to the Creator. The brain may not be in place immediately after conception, but "The human brain begins forming very early in prenatal life (just three weeks after conception), but in many ways, brain development is a lifelong project."[29] Soon after fertilization of the ovum, thinking begins at least at the level of genes, and it never stops after that.

As St. Basil wrote, "the operation of the mind is wonderful… in its perpetual motion…" Thinking is man's essential characteristic; it is aptly described by the words "perennial motion." We will never know how much time and energy of that perennial motion each human being dedicates to sexuality. Ohio State University researchers found that the average man thinks about sex 20 times a day or less;" whatever their definition of "average man" is.

The frequency with which human beings think about sex has been debated since time immemorial, but continuously changing variables make it impossible to know the answer.

One thing is true: the teleology of human sexuality is no longer merely what Darwinian Evolution developed in us eons ago. The omnipotent, ever-present Creative Energy of Love that Christians call the Third Person in God, revolutionized and redefined human sexuality upon impregnating a virgin.

We shall revisit the myth of the Annunciation that sparked the only true revolution human sexuality has experienced. At this point it is sufficient to say that from the moment that event took place until now, human sexuality is more than the mere result of biological evolution.

Dorothy L. Sayers was only one of recent and not-so-recent thinkers to reiterate that "Love is the

Energy of creation" (above, page 21). Echoing Aristotle's *Nicomachean Ethics*, "Love is like activity;"[30] the Spanish philosopher José Ortega y Gasset wrote "everything is action in Love" (*en el amor todo es actividad*).[31] In a statement that seems to contradict the rest of his book, *The Little Book of Atheist Spirituality*, André Comte-Sponville writes: "The absolute is not love; rather, love can open us to the absolute" (page 206).

In other words, Love is the Omnipotent. One can find countless quotes to illustrate the relation of human sexuality to Love. The Virgin Mary's revolution of our sexuality revealed the true nature of human erotic love activity: from being a mere biological reproductive system, human sexuality became the most important and spiritual manifestation of the creative Energy of Love:

"Let him kiss me with the kisses of his mouth.
  Your love is more delightful than wine;
    delicate is the fragrance of your perfume,
  Your name is an oil poured out,
    and that is why the maidens love you
  Draw me in your footsteps, let us run.
  The King has brought me into his rooms;
    you will be our joy and our gladness.
  We shall praise your love above wine;
    how right it is to love you."   --*The Song of Songs*

Chapter 9

# Erotic Love

G. Klimt, The Kiss.

Only once in its entire history has human sexuality experienced a true revolution: it was triggered by the story of a Jewish teenaged girl two millennia ago.

How could such a moment happen?

It took millions of years for Evolution to develop the marvelous human reproductive system. Some biologists are of the opinion that the survival instinct results from the evolution of the genome of each species. As the human brain developed, it acquired characteristics that enabled it to specialize and compartmentalize its operations.

Transmission of genetic information became more and more sophisticated, producing very complex activities    such as language, memory, intelligence, self-awareness, independence from natural forces, and so on. Scientist Stephen Meyer investigates these matters in his work, *Signature in the Cell*:

> "But if this is true, how did the information in the DNA arise? Is this striking appearance of design the product of actual design or of a natural process that can mimic the powers of a *designing intelligence*?"[32]

Can Darwinian evolution produce wisdom? When and how does man's *knowledge* become *wisdom*? Did wisdom bring into existence social institutions like the family, religion, laws, and social groupings? We can only affirm that evolution guaranteed the survival of the human species thanks to these societal entities.

Scientists may be correct estimating millions of years of Evolution to prepare the human brain for rational and not merely instinctive operations.

Questions remain, however: are my intelligence and my free will products of Evolution, or do they point to an act of creation in the Present, outside of time and space?

Understanding and/or choosing a course of action, the 'aha or eureka' moments; are these temporal, physiological operations? Or do intelligence and free will point to a spiritual nature operating in the non-temporal Present? Such spiritual activities presuppose the continuous presence of a source of spiritual Energy, different from and in control of Evolution.

Each human being is always present in his own process of becoming from its beginning to its end; does that fact replicate or simulate the continuous presence of a Creative Being in the process of cosmic evolution?

These questions and their answers have constituted the substance of philosophical and theological arguments since recorded history. They denote a physical and a metaphysical understanding of Creation: one observes the evolution of matter, the other sees above and beyond matter.

At this point, the two words, *sexuality* and *revolution* bear some explaining. Let us begin with *sexuality*. Evolution produced all vegetative and animal reproductive systems in Nature. Essential to the human reproductive system is bisexual complementation, which, as Aristotle explained,

> " [is] the production of another like itself, an animal producing an animal, a plant a plant, in order that, as far as its nature allows, it may partake in the eternal and divine."[33]

In human sexuality one spermatozoid and one ovum fuse to provide the new creature's body, the means by which each of us may or may not come to exist. A fertilized egg endowed with its own principle of motion — that is, its be*ing* — is a new *human life*. If the fertilized egg is not endowed thusly, Nature follows its evolutionary course and discards the lifeless matter.

Once the temporal, material process of becoming has begun, a human being is present to it. That specific human being is created to begin, sustain, and bring to its end (*telos*) that specific process. An immaterial entity - the *new being - animates* a specific matter, the fertilized ovum. Human *becoming* takes time and space whereas a human *being* cannot be but in the Present.

We can now attempt to clarify the meaning of *revolution*. It is *a substantial alteration to the process of Evolution.* Nicolas Copernicus introduced the term in his famous treatise *De Revolutionibus orbium coelestium* (1543) which triggered the Copernican Revolution. It effected a substantial and transcendental alteration in our understanding of the Cosmos. Actually, there was no such alteration; Copernicus simply described the Cosmos more accurately.

For an authentic revolution to occur, catalytic events are required: a revolution of sexuality is no exception. These catalysts share similar characteristics, for example:

- they are found among the least powerful social groups:
- they produce substantial alterations in their societies and the alterations enjoy a longevity that depends on the entity that causes it;
- the catalysts use an Energy *not found in time /space.*

Some events seem to satisfy our definition of revolution but few of them actually transformed anything or anyone *substantially* or for a significant period of time. The socio-political history of France for example, experienced substantial alterations at the end of the eighteenth century. A "revolutionary" crowd of Parisians stormed the Bastille prison; this event marked a substantial alteration to the government of that nation. From an absolute monarchy, France became a republic.

These events led to the creation of First Republic and a true revolution seemed a *fait accompli*. Two historical facts frustrated the French Revolution: first, its cause was a mob, devoid of sufficient *intelligence* to assure its success, and secondly, it lasted only until Napoleon Bonaparte put an end to it. Once again the truth of Thomas Jefferson's words was confirmed: "The generation which commences a revolution rarely completes it."

The October Revolution in Russia was another alteration of the socio-political structures of a nation that seem to satisfy the definition of "revolution." In fact, the violent events that took place in October of 1917 were but a phase of the Russian Revolution. Like the Parisian mobs over a century earlier, Russian workers and peasants led by Vladimir Lenin replaced the Czarist rule with Marxist ideologues identifying themselves as leaders of the working class.

Civil strife ensued and Lenin became a dictator until his death in 1924. Joseph Stalin succeeded him, until his own death in 1953. Even though the Soviet leaders' power lasted eight decades, they failed to revolutionize the government structure: the Czars' authoritarianism was replaced by that of the Soviet hierarchy. From the rule of the Czarist regime to that of the dictators and the Presidents of the Russian Federation, absolute power remained absolute power; *plus ça change, plus c'est la même chose*....

The American colonists' break from the British Crown comes closer to satisfying the conditions of a true revolution. Firstly, the ultimate Energy that animated their cause did not come from their own history but from their faith in their Creator: the source of their power was not found in time/space. Secondly, the success and longevity of the American Revolution was assured when its leaders accepted "...the separate and equal station to which *the Laws of Nature* and of *Nature's God* entitle them..." (Declaration of Independence).

CHAPTER 10

# THE ONE AND ONLY TRUE SEXUAL REVOLUTION.

Two thousand years ago, the bi-sexual reproductive system of human beings experienced an authentic revolution. The story of the event that caused it, the Annunciation, is told below (Chapter 11). In it:

- The protagonists of the story were among the least powerful members of their social groups;
- the human reproductive system was forever changed among those of us who joined the sexual revolution announced to Mary;
- and, most importantly, the Energy that triggers and sustains the one and only revolution of human sexuality is not created: it is perennially in the Present.

Human intelligence is limited by time and space; to transcend it, faith is needed. Faith — that reality transcends time and space, faith that we are in the present, and faith that human intelligence constantly manifests the invisible and imperceptible "now."

Each of us is free to accept or reject faith, but, contrary to Richard Dawkins' definition, faith is not "belief without evidence."[34] Rather, as Saint Augustine explained 1600 years earlier, "…you believe because you do not understand, and by believing you become apt to understand."[35]

Faith enables us to understand and interpret the various revelation stories; revelations *about* and *in* the perennial Present. That faith enables human intelligence to see through (*intus-legere*) the temporal manifestations of the ever present Creator. Such faith is unnecessary whenever and wherever the temporal manifestations themselves are equated to their Eternal Creator.[36] In such cases there is no need for intelligence: the temporal manifestations themselves are *idols to be obeyed blindly*, without the benefit of reasoning or free will.

The Present reveals itself *through* each instant of the time/space continuum, i.e., in Evolution. Humans are the only intelligent creatures capable of seeing into the revelation myths. The past and the future are perceptible to our time-operated senses, the former by memory and the latter by imagination. Knowledge of the Present, on the other hand, is not sensorial since it is not part of time. Awareness of the Present requires an individual's act of faith.

Alterations to the Evolutionary process — sometimes called "miracles — have occurred constantly since its very beginning: they transcend the time/ space continuum.[37] *Our experience of Eternity — being in the Present — is the genesis of our faith, not the lack of evidence.*

Now we can ask: what does the Virgin Mary's Annunciation story reveal to us? How is it that it revolutionized human sexuality?

Fra Angelico, Annunciation, 1437-46

## CHAPTER 11

# THE ANNUNCIATION MYTH

Mary's story of the Annunciation according to the apostle Luke, 1, 26-38:

"In the sixth month the angel Gabriel was sent by God to a town in Galilee called Nazareth, 27 to a virgin betrothed to a man named Joseph, of the House of David; and and the virgin's name was Mary. 28He went in and said to her, 'Rejoice, you who enjoy God's favor! The Lord is with you.'29 She was deeply disturbed by these words and asked herself what this greeting could mean, [30] but the angel said to her, 'Mary, do not be afraid; you have won God's favour.[31] Look! You are to conceive in your womb and bear a son, and you must name him Jesus.[32] He will be great and will be called Son of the Most High. The Lord God will give him the throne of his ancestor David; [33] he will rule over the House of Jacob forever and his reign will have no end.'[34]

Mary said to the angel, 'But how can this come about, since I have no knowledge of man?'[35] The angel answered, 'The Holy Spirit will come upon you, and the power of the Most High will cover you with its shadow. And so the child will be holy and will be called Son of God.[36] And I tell you this too: your cousin Elizabeth also, in her old age, has conceived a son, and she whom people called barren is now in her sixth month,[37] for nothing is impossible to God.'[38] Mary said, 'You see before you the Lord's servant, let it happen to me as you have said.' And the angel left her."

(Joseph's story, *Matthew*, 1; 18-25)

18 This is how Jesus Christ came to be born. His mother Mary was betrothed to Joseph; but before they came to live together she was found to be with child through the Holy Spirit.[19] Her husband Joseph, being an upright man and wanting to spare her disgrace, decided to divorce her informally.[20] He had made up up his mind to do this when suddenly the angel of the Lord appeared to him in a dream and said, 'Joseph son of David, do not be afraid to take Mary home as your wife, because she has conceived what is in her by the Holy Spirit.[21] She will give birth to a son and you must name him Jesus, because he is the one who is to save his people from their sins.' [22] Now all this took place to fulfill what the Lord had spoken through the prophet: Look! the virgin is with child and will give birth to a son whom they will call Immanuel, a name which means 'God-is-with-us'. [24] When Joseph woke up he did what the angel of the Lord had told him to do: he took his wife to his home; [25] he had not had intercourse with her when she gave birth to a son; and he named him Jesus."

Mary's and Joseph's stories triggered the Virgin's revolution of human sexuality. The event has been depicted by hundreds of artists through the ages. Fra Angelico's fresco in San Marco, Florence, dates from almost six centuries ago.

**Paolo de Matteis, The Annunciation, 1712**

Four hundred and fifty years later the myth behind the monk's painting was retold by the Oscar Wilde in his poem (1881) *Ave Maria Plena Gratia*, which ends with this thought:

"And now with wondering eyes and heart I stand
Before this supreme mystery of Love:
A kneeling girl with passionless pale face,
An angel with a lily in his hand,
And over both with outstretched wings the Dove".

Many ancient myths[38] foretold the contemporary Darwinian hypothesis of human sexuality and procreation. The most familiar to many of us is found in *Genesis*: "And God created man in his own image, and He created them male and female" (1, 27). In this story, God commanded Adam and Eve to procreate and multiply *His own image,* humanity. The Creator's unity is reflected not in the male or the female, but in the unity of all human beings and also in that unity found in each one of us. "They are of one heart and of one mind with us in the Lord" (Paulinus to St. Augustine).

Almost two decades ago, Pope John Paul II reminded the world of the need to be one with the Son of God:

"*Ut unum sint!* The call for Christian unity made by the Second Vatican Council with such impassioned commitment is finding an ever greater echo in the hearts of believers, especially as the Year 2000 approaches, a year which Christians will celebrate as a sacred Jubilee, the comemoration of the Incarnation of the Son of God, who became man in order to save *humanity*."[39]

Those who accept the Virgin Mother's revolution learn the name of the new-born humanity: the Mystical Body of Christ.

Another myth that illustrates the stage at which human sexuality had arrived five centuries before that of the Annunciation is found in Plato:

"At this Zeus took counsel with the other gods as to what was to be done. They found themselves in a rather awkward situation...At last, however, after racking his brains, Zeus offered a solution. I think I can see my way, he said, to put an end to this disturbance by weakening these people without destroying them. What I propose to do is to cut them in half, thus killing two birds with one stone, for each one will be only half as strong ..."

*Symposium*,190 C-D

Themes similar to the *Genesis* account are also found in Plato's text: the creation of man and woman by dividing the original androgynous creature into two, the nostalgia for the original essential unity, and the direct intervention into the creative process of a god (For Aristophanes that god is Zeus).

Both myths depict human beings as individually incomplete: their existential perfection can be restored only by being faithful to the dictates of their Maker. In *Genesis*, these include man's control over Nature ("Be masters of the fish of the sea, the birds of heaven," etc.) and over himself ("of the tree of the knowledge of good and evil, you are not to eat").

In another Platonic dialogue, the **Theaetetus,** we also find divine plans for humans:

> "SOCRATES: There are two patterns eternally set before them; the one blessed and divine, the other godless and wretched: but they do not see them, or perceive that in their utter folly and infatuation they are growing like the one and unlike the other, by reason of their evil deeds" (176a-).

How are we to understand these and other myths that describe the divine creation of human beings?

Different nations produce different folklore and cultural perspectives, and yet, when referring to the human condition, they reveal common essential traits. One of those traits is our ability to read into ancient myths and to substantiate (*sub-stans*, Latin for under-standing) their meaning.

Human activities are prescribed by natural evolution but are also eternally "blessed and divine." In Socrates' words, human sexuality developed according to "two patterns eternally set before them; the one blessed and divine, the other godless and wretched." But "patterns set eternally" and concepts like "blessed and divine" have *meaning* exclusively for *humans.* We are the only living creatures capable of interpreting "patterns set eternally."

Some 22 centuries after Plato, Charles Darwin described the patterns of biological evolution found in Nature in his *On the Origin of Species* (1859). Following the dictates of nature, male and female human beings reproduced and multiplied the species. Their metaphysical nature was revealed by the operations of human intelligence and free will.

St. Augustine of Hippo by Sandro Botticelli,
*fides quaerens intellectum* (St. Anselm).

## CHAPTER 12

# FAITH, REASON, AND LOVE

One atheist's opinion notwithstanding, faith is not "belief without evidence." Abundant literature has been written by those who hold that faith diminishes or hinders the operation of human intelligence. On the other hand, Plato, Aristotle, Saint Augustine, and others have understood the essential role of faith in human cognition: "...you believe because you do not understand, and by believing you become apt to understand."

Examples of basic human faith include belief in the Future, since we cannot know that which is not; belief in the Present, since we cannot experience it except as a memory of the immediate past; and, most ironically, the set of beliefs implicit in the scientific method, based on experiments that require faith in their future results.

Simply put, our existence is one continuous act of faith that begins at conception and ends at death. *I am becoming who I am*: the affirmation "I am" entails belief in the imperceptible reality of one's being-in-the-Present; "becoming" presupposes faith in the disappearance of the non-existent Future (nothing), into the no-longer-existent Past (nothing). The end (*telos*) of becoming—"who I am"—entails one's faith that the same being-in-the-Present that began the process remains in the Present, through time and space, forever.

### Jacques Derrida's "being-towards-death"

Physical death, the ultimate act of faith, is universally accepted. All of us *believe* in physical death even though none of us has ever experienced it. The actuality of physical death can be predicted because our intelligence sees beyond the ephemeral appearance of life. The French philosopher Derrida writes:

"It is in the being-towards-death that the self is constituted in each case, comes into its own, that is, comes to realize its unsubstitutability. *The identity of the oneself is given by death.*"[40]

In other words, physical death presupposes faith that our Maker's Spirit ultimately enlightens our intelligence and free will to reveal our identity, in the Present, liberated from all temporal encumbrances.

American philosopher Jacob Needleman writes:

"That brings me to this other question of the unknown: death…None of us knows how we're going to be in front of that. It is almost always terrifying, of course. But it is possible… to experience an energy for a moment that's outside of time, It is timeless. It's unborn. It's undying. Even if you touch that only for a second, you know that there is *something else*. Something else independent of time that you didn't know about. That's the great unknown…"[41]

As of its first manifestation, human intelligence continuously reads through the temporal process of *becoming, discovering the being that sustains it.* In the words of biologist Meyer, "…the [genetic] information necessary to the first life, like the information in human technology or literature, arose from a designing intelligence" (*Signature in the Cell*, 17).

This genetic epistemology indicates that Derrida's "being-towards-death" is present in the fertilized egg or "first life" in *utero materno*. Each new spiritual agent (each "who I am", each soul) is different from that of its parents. The newly created being uses spiritual means (intelligence and free will) to identify itself, i.e., the being that animates it.[42]

### Bruce F. Barton, What Can a Man Believe?

Human intelligence is an immaterial activity that always occurs in the never-ending Present. Spiritual activities — intelligence and free will — do not result from Cosmic Evolution (i.e., time/space). Bruce F. Barton (1886-1967), a twentieth century American successful in business and in politics, a "Renaissance" man, was also a gifted writer capable of explaining complex theological and philosophical topics.[43] In *What can a man believe?* (1927), Barton explained the relation of intelligence to faith:

> "Because I have intelligence, there must be Intelligence behind the Universe. Why? Because otherwise the universe has created something greater than itself, for it has created me; and the assumption that the lesser can produce the greater, that something can come out of nothing, does

> violence to my common sense. I cannot conceive or accept it. In other words, *because I am, I believe God is.*"[44]

Pope John Paul II's encyclical *Fides et Ratio* (1998) also clarifies the epistemological importance of faith in our own times. Evolution did not create itself: only a power different from it can create and sustain it.

By contrast, the most recent dogmatisms of physicist Stephen Hawkins are scientifically improvable statements of absurd irrational beliefs:[45]

> "Because there is a law such as gravity, the universe can and will create    itself from nothing," he writes. "Spontaneous creation is the reason there is something rather than nothing, why the universe exists, why we exist."[46]

Hawkins' musings illustrate Richard Dawkin's definition of faith; "belief without evidence."

Artificial intelligence was designed and made by something other than itself, namely, human intelligence. In turn, human intelligence was designed and created by something other than itself, to wit, Divine Intelligence. A Divine Creator designed and created natural Evolution: This Creator's Energy is present at the origin of Creation; This Energy is the power of the "Big Bang"; the continued expansion of time and space is sustained by the ever Present Energy of the Creator; the Creator's Energy continuously creates time and space.

Ironically, people who deliberately reject the truth and beauty expressed in most myths are themselves not to be believed. Is it reasonable to deny the action of a transcendental Creator based on the inadequacies of the creation myths? Movie producer Paul Verhoeven (*American Psycho, Pulp Fiction*) pretends to do just that. Rather than believe and benefit from Jesus' story and that of the Virgin Mary, Verhoeven chooses to rewrite it: "Jesus might have been the product of his mother being raped by a Roman soldier."[47] The truth and beauty of the original story are thus deliberately and maliciously deleted.

With a clearer notion of the relation between faith and intelligence we can better understand mythological languages. The myth of Narcissus is a good example. No one accepts the story as history, but all agree that it illustrates a common human trait; love of one's *image* instead of oneself may be fatal.

### Understanding the Myth of the Annunciation

To understand and benefit from the myth of the Annunciation, the story Mary told over two thousand years ago must be believed. There are people who resent the very existence of myths, but as G. K. Chesterton wrote:

> "This is the mighty and branching tree called mythology which ramifies round the whole world, whose remote branches under separate skies bear like colored birds the costly idols of Asia and the half-baked fetishes of Africa and the fairy kings and princesses of the folk-tales of the forest, and buried amid vines and olives the Lares of the Latins, and carried on the clouds of Olympus the buoyant supremacy of the gods of Greece. These are the myths: and *he who has no sympathy with myths has no sympathy with men.*"[48]

The Virgin Mary's story triggered the one true and beautiful revolution of human sexuality. We begin to appreciate the profound meaning of her story once we describe one of its consequences: human sexuality is no longer defined merely by physical and biological teleology. Whether this young virgin was narrating a true and beautiful experience, or spinning the fact that she had become pregnant, belies its real meaning.

The importance and value of the Annunciation story lies in its significance to those who believe it. Was Mary lying about her pregnancy? Was she protecting her future husband? What changes visited her family after the Annunciation? Who experienced them? Could these events result merely from natural evolution?

Faith illuminates intelligence and enables it to understand and interpret revelations *of what is,* that which is, always, in the perennial Present. The Annunciation story depicts how the omnipotent Divine Energy, ever Present in Creation, manifested itself to an unwed Jewish girl two millennia ago. Belief in the story depends on the credibility of its source and on one's spiritual life.

The Virgin Mary gave total faith to the Source of the request. She was not naïve, she simply believed that the omnipotence of her Creator's Divine Energy could impregnate her were she to consent to His will. And so it happened; Mary conceived a child, so the myth goes, *not according to the natural law* of biological Evolution, bi-sexually, but by the direct intervention in her womb of the Supernatural Energy of Love. We *are free to accept or not the illumination of faith* in the Father to understand the myth. Mary herself had to choose: was the apparition the Almighty's messenger real or was it the product of adolescent infatuation?

"Let it be done unto me according to thy Word"; upon her submission to the messenger's words, a real sexual revolution had begun. The first consequence was evident: erotic love was God's love.[49] At least the following realities were simultaneously revealed: 1) sexual consummation was not essential to the sacrament of marriage, and

2) the procreation commanded by God was that of Himself in the Person of His Son.

At the Annunciation, Mary's story began the revolution of social institutions such as marriage, family, maternity, and their relationship to religious and political power structures. Later, Jesus verified the story of the young Virgin and the unknown Father.

Mary's myth revealed the true nature and identity of Love; in Plato's words, "the first of all the gods." God can and does manifest Himself directly and through His creatures to all humans, thus, there is no reason to disbelieve the myth behind Virgin's pregnancy. Mary redefined the role of sexuality outside the parameters of biology. For instance, the domination inherited genetically from our alpha-male simian ancestors would end upon accepting Mary's story. The enlightenment of our intelligence by the Creator's faith is essentially necessary to accept and interpret his word (*Logos*).

"His highest divine attribute is His creativeness and that which is creative exists always in the beginning stage. God is eternally in *Genesis*. Each time He lifts his gaze He sees chaos and He wants to create order. But creation is coupling and God must come together with His female aspects to produce birth."

--Isaac Bashevis Singer, [50]

"In the Church we discover that the life of each human being is a story of love,"[51] and God is Love.     --Pope Benedict XVI

# PART II

# RESTORING HUMAN SEXUALITY

Part II is about the revolutionary consequences that followed Mary's acceptance of her Divine Lover's proposal. At the Annunciation, Mary agreed to become the mother of Love's begotten Son. From that instant forward, human complementary sexuality — the result of biological evolution — becomes primarily a manifestation of Love/*eros*[52], the Word of God.

The Virgin Mary's *fiat* transformed the breeding of humans into a secondary manifestation of God's eternal Word, a *possibility — not an actuality*. The Incarnation of the Word — Love — is the primary end of the Virgin's motherhood.

CHAPTER 1

# SEXUALITY TODAY

A sexist, misogynist, *machista* culture prevails in the world today.[53] This situation may be even worse in the United States, in part due to the misinterpretation of basic concepts of freedom and happiness found in its Constitution and in the Bill of Rights. The Constitution states that "The blessings of Liberty" derive from the will of the People and from their "more perfect union." Then the First Amendment seems to negate that statement, assigning "All legislative Powers" not to "We the People" but to Congress.

Actually, neither the People nor the Congress is the source of "the blessings of Liberty." Why did the signers of the Constitution (1787) and of the Bill of Rights (1789) dismiss what had been agreed to in the Declaration of Independence (1776)? Then, it was evident to everyone that the "Laws of Nature and Nature's God" endowed us "with certain unalienable Rights, that among these are Life, Liberty and the pursuit of Happiness."

The notion of happiness mentioned in the Declaration of Independence is directly referred to "Nature's God," not to "We the People," and much less to the Congress.

Thomas Jefferson's "pursuit of happiness" shows a clear affinity to the Utilitarian ideology of British philosopher Jeremy Bentham (1748-1832), of James Mill, and his son, John Stuart Mill (1806-1873).

In *A Fragment on Government* (1776), Bentham wrote: "it is the greatest happiness of the greatest number that is the measure of right and wrong." Later, John Stuart Mill's *Utilitarianism* (1863) affirms that

> "The *creed* which accepts as the foundation of morals, Utility, or the Greatest-Happiness Principle, holds that actions are right in proportion as they tend to promote happiness, wrong as they tend to produce the reverse of happiness."

Up to this point, utilitarianism serves Jefferson's Declaration of Independence, but Mill's "creed" goes on to define "happiness" in terms that deny "Nature's God:"

> "By happiness is intended pleasure, and the absence of pain; by unhappiness, pain, and the privation of pleasure."

This materialistic ethic combined with the puritanical beliefs of the early colonialists to create false notions of freedom and happiness, especially in the area of sexuality. Along with a misunderstood notion of Adam Smith's *laissez faire* economic theories (*The Wealth of Nations*, 1776), the Utilitarian definition of happiness produced a degenerate attitude toward sexuality.

Today, sex has become little more than a trading commodity.[54] This attitude peaked during the 1960's when major religions, cults, and a number of secular institutions propagated the idea that human sexuality is justified only as a means to achieve biological reproduction or as a commercial transaction.

Very few people acknowledge the essential reason to activate their sexuality, namely, to express the Divine Presence in each of us, and to manifest Love:

> "My beloved spoke, and said unto me:
> 'Rise up, my love, my fair one, and come away."[55]

**Bernini, Ste. Therese's Ecstasy, Rome**

**CHAPTER 2**

# RESTORING EROS

"So the question is not whether we will be extremists, but what kind of extremists: will we be extremists for hate or for love?"[56] The Virgin Mary was an "extremist" for Love. Her response to God's messenger was possible and believable only if given by a human being capable of extreme Love: "'You see before you the Lord's servant, let it happen to me as you have said.' This unity with God "creates love, a unity in which both God and man remain themselves yet become fully one,"[57] as should happen in all erotic manifestations of Love.

Mary's submission to our Creator at the Annunciation revealed the revolutionary new law of Love that substituted the old. A simple law it was, capable of being understood by an *almah*, a teenager from Nazareth over two thousand years ago. Like Dr. King twenty centuries later, the Virgin Mary was an "extremist for love" in her own society; both of them risked their lives doing God's will. The Virgin Mary rejected customs, traditions, and no longer valid laws in order to become pregnant by her Lover, with whom "nothing is impossible."

Mary's consent transcended time and space. The Virgin Mother's assent is essential to **God**'s New Covenant, the Mystical Body of Christ, as it was foreseen from all eternity.[58] Her story is a clear sign of the Creator's omnipotence.

Mary's pregnancy was, in her Jewish culture, a crime, punishable by death. So serious was her situation that her fiancé Joseph was willing to spare her social shame by breaking up their unconsummated marriage. The Old Law was clear: "Unlawful intercourse with a woman betrothed to a man was adultery, because the betrothed woman was deemed as inviolable as the married woman. The punishment for this crime was stoning to death at the place of public execution."[59] Joseph may have been the first to believe the Virgin Mary's mythological explanation of her pregnancy.

Such punishments to women for sexual offences continue in the twenty-first century, as shown in the following examples:

Islam: "The fornicatress [*sic*] and the fornicator, flog each of them. Let no pity withhold you in their case, in a punishment prescribed by Allah, if you believe in Allah and the Last Day. And let a party of the believers witness their punishment. (This punishment is for unmarried persons guilty of the above crime, but if married persons commit it (illegal sex), the punishment is to stone them to death, according to Allah's Law). *Qur'an*, Sura 24 (An-Nur).

China: "The case of Deng Yujiao. She stabbed to death a drunken local official who was trying to rape her in 2009 but was charged with intentional assault. A massive public outcry pressure authorities to release her without punishment."[60] To this day, women's lives and those of their children are constantly imperiled everywhere in the world.[61]

Jesus dedicated his life to implementing the revolution that his mother had begun at the Annunciation. By letting someone other than her betrothed sire her child, Mary had rebelled against the old Law. The birth of Jesus signaled Mary's victory over the '*ancien régime*.' The Law of Love was promulgated—so the story goes—in a stable, among animals and a few witnesses: it superseded the Law given to Moses. Later, Elizabeth recognized "the mother of my Lord" when she greeted Mary, her cousin. The Virgin Mother knew her new-born infant would restore the Kingdom of God on Earth; she told the good news to the mother of John the Baptist, "My soul proclaims the greatness of the Lord!"[62]

Years later, the "transfiguration" of the old laws was announced at Cana: "[Saint] John is careful to note that Jesus' first miracle (at Cana) is done in response to Mary's intercession."[63] Concern for her friends' happiness prompted Mary to tell her Son they had run out of wine: he could remedy their problem. Was running out of wine so insignificant as to justify Jesus' comment to his mother, "Woman, why turn to me?" The incident and the water-into-wine miracle acquire transcendental significance when put in the wider context of Jesus' message. The wedding feast at Cana foretells His union with the Church; the water/wine become symbols of His death ("one of the soldiers pierced Jesus' side with a spear, brining a sudden flow of blood and water") and of the Eucharist; and the wedding feast reminds us of Mary's intimacy with Jesus' Father. The revelation made to Mary of the New Law of Love was made public, at a feast celebrating conjugal love, the sacrament of union between Jesus and his Mystical Body.

CHAPTER 3

# JESUS RESTORES LOVE

Jesus explained the new Law: Love one another. His resolution of the case against the adulterous woman exemplified how the New Law is to be applied in the New Israel. The New Law is one of forgiveness and life everlasting rather than one of punishment and bodily death:

> "'If there is one of you who has not sinned,' Jesus tells the scribes and Pharisees, 'let him be the first to throw a stone at her' ... When they heard this they went away one by one, beginning with the eldest, until Jesus was left alone with the woman, who remained standing there. He looked up and said, 'Woman, where are they? Has no one condemned you?' 'No one, sir' she replied. 'Neither do I condemn you,' said Jesus 'go away, and don't sin anymore.'"[64]

At the Annunciation "the order of Love" was revealed to humanity: the Son of the Almighty Creator proclaimed the new order *in aeternum*, *now and forever*. Jesus' life, death, and resurrection confirmed the veracity of His mother's story, God was his Father. God was *always* with him: "The Father and I are one."[65]

Each of our parents participated in bringing us into time and space. Spiritually, existentially, they witnessed God's act of creating/sustaining a being, a human soul, where before, there was none.[66] It is not our parents' participation in God's creative act that sustains our [human] being in time and space; it is the presence of the Father that keeps us in eternity, until the end of our time.

As poet William Wordsworth put it:

"My heart leaps up when I behold
A rainbow in the sky;
*So was it when my life began;*
*So is it now that I am a man;*
*So be it when I shall grow old,*
*Or let me die!*
The Child is father of the Man;
And I could wish my days to be
Bound each to each by natural piety."[67]

## The Presence of the Father

"The power of the Most High shall overshadow you," and as of the moment God's messenger spoke those words, His Word begat a human being in Mary's womb. God's Son *is* Mary's revelation. The number of those who reject the Virgin Mother's story has increased, as well as the number of those who realize that their parents' presence never leaves them. Regardless of particular circumstances, Shakespeare's words, "I am thy father's spirit"[68] will always resonate in each one of us.

Fustel de Coulanges explained the significance of a father's never-ending presence in a family in these terms:

> "In the rigor of primitive law, the sons remained attached to the father's hearth, and, consequently, subject to his authority; *while he lived* they were minors."[69]

Sigmund Freud attested to his continued attachment to his own father in *The Interpretation of Dreams* (1900), acknowledging that a father's death "is the most important event, the most poignant loss, of a man's life."[70]

God the Father was forever present in the Virgin Mary, and that presence begot their son, Jesus.

### Divine Creation and Human Beings

Historical, fictional, or scientific myths, can be detrimental to humanity. For example, some scientists believe the myth that reality consists only of matter and energy, denying the existence of spiritu-al elements. The "Big Bang" theory of creation is one such scientific myth:

> "Because there is a law such as gravity, the universe can and will create itself *from nothing*. Spontaneous creation is the reason there is something rather than nothing, why the universe exists, why we exist."[71]

Fortunately, more rational explanations of Creation are available. In St. Thomas Aquinas' words:

> "It ought to be said that God does not produce things into being by one operation and conserve them in being by another. The being [ESSE] of permanent things is not divisible, except accidentally as it is subject to some motion; being, however, exists in the instant. Therefore the operation of God does not differ according as it makes the beginning of being (*alpha*) and as it makes the continuation of being (*omega*)."[72]

Creation and conservation are the same divine act, because the being of the creature is the same throughout the existence of the creature.[73] To deny divine intervention in the creation of human beings negates our supernatural origin and end.[74]

Myths found in other cultures also tell us about the intervention of divinities in the creation of human beings. The *Holy Qur'an,* for instance, tells us: "…And Allah has brought you forth from earth? [*alpha*]. He will return you into the earth and bring you forth (at Resurrection)? [*omega*]."[75] The best known story of the creation of man in Greek mythology is that of the god Prometheus who formed man out of mud. Athena, a virgin daughter of Zeus, breathed life into the lifeless mud.

In the Western Hemisphere, the Maya story of the first men is told in the *Popol Vuh*: after repeated failed attempts—first with wood and then with mud—the gods Tepeu and Gucumatz fashioned their own race of worshippers out of maize *masa* (corn dough).

In Hinduism, Brahma is the god (***deva***) of creation. Reminiscent of the Christian Triune God, Brahma is one of three, the others being Visṇu, the omnipotent Preserver of Creation, and Śiva, the Destroyer and Transformer, among other titles. According to the *Siva Purana*, Brahma is the father of Manu, and from Manu all human beings are descended. In the *Purana*, Brahma said, "I was then prompted by Siva, present within me, and hence I split myself into two, one had the form of a woman and the other half that of a man."

Was Plato familiar with this Hindu story? "What I propose to do is to cut them in half, thus killing two birds with one stone, for each one will be only half as strong ...."[76]

To summarize: the participation of one or more divinities is a common element in most creation myths in the world. The beginning of the Universe and of our individual beings points to a supernatural, a-temporal or eternal origin (AΩ). As St. Augustine put it:

> "O Lord, since you are outside time in eternity, are you unaware of the things that I tell you? Or do you see in time the things that occur in it?"[77]

This divine Source is the foundation of natural societies: it leads us to the revolutionary freedom found only in the "order of Love" announced by the Virgin Mary. To ignore the divine Source condemns us to the slavery of the senses.

"When [the Church] baptizes a child,' wrote John Donne in 1623:

> "that action concerns me; for that child is thereby connected to that body (AΩ) whereof I am a member. And when she buries a man, that action concerns me: *all mankind is of one author* and is one volume..."[78]

From the *Missal of Bernhard von Rohr,
Archbishop of Salzburg* ca.1481.

CHAPTER 4

# THE NEW EVE

The Virgin Mary's consent to God's messenger allowed Him to engender in her "that body whereof" membership is humanity at large, the Mystical Body of Christ.[79]  The Virgin's Son "is definitely the Way and the Life, the *halaqa*, by which *humanity* walks according to a divine program."[80]

All religions adapt their belief systems to the principalities of this world,[81] sometimes with tragic consequences to believers and non-believers alike.

As long as humans fail to transcend their temporal existence, they will ignore what C. S. Lewis called "the next step" of their Evolution: "When is *the thing beyond man* going to appear?"[82] The true identity of humanity at large" is discovered only when we acknowledge that there is a "divinity that shapes our ends."[83]

The birth of the Church occurred at Pentecost. As had happened to Mary at the Annunciation, she and Jesus' disciples "were all filled with the Holy Spirit. They began to speak in foreign languages as the Spirit gave them the gift of speech."[84] Speaking in foreign tongues is a clear sign of acculturation. The spread of Christianity immediately after Jesus Christ's death and resurrection could not have taken place without the Hellenization of its good news:

> "The language question was by no means an irrelevant matter. With the Greek language a whole world of concepts, categories of thought, inherited metaphors, and subtle connotations of meaning enters Christian thought."[85]

Acculturation was already implied in the Virgin Mother's command to the servants at the wedding feast in Cana, "Do whatever He tells you."[86]

The events described at the feast of Pentecost and the controversies that followed regarding who could be a member of the Mystical Body, confirm that Jesus' message transcends all cultures and customs. Luke, for instance, wrote as a Gentile for Gentile Christians; his gospel manifests a mastery of the Greek language as well as familiarity with Jewish sources. The same must be said of Saint Paul whose understanding of evangelization clashed so much with that of Saint Peter and other apostles that they had to convene the first Church Council in Jerusalem.

To this day, Christian evangelists adapt their teachings to their audiences, as Saint Francis Xavier did in India:

> "We could not understand one another, as I spoke Castilian and they Malabar; so I picked out the most intelligent and well-read of them, and then sought out with the greatest diligence men who knew both languages. We held meetings for several days and by our joint efforts and with infinite difficulty we translated the Catechism into the Malabar tongue."[87]

Moments before his death and as a gesture of his love, Jesus declares the Virgin Mary mother of his Mystical Body: "'Woman, this is your son.' Then to the disciple he said, 'This is your mother'."[88]    The full context of those words includes Jesus' ear lier definition of who are his true kinsmen: "'My mother and my brothers are those who hear the word of God and put it into practice.'"[89]

At Pentecost, Mary is spiritually impregnated once more by God's Creative Spirit; this time she becomes the mother of the Mystical Body of Christ, the Church. The New Law revealed at Mount Golgotha replaced the Old Law given to Moses at Mount Sinai. By giving birth to her Son's Mystical Body, the new Eve, *restores* us to our original state, sons of God the Father.

Mary's myth is the story of the restoration of humanity.[90] We are no longer bound by the Old Covenant laws: now and forever, we are His "friends." not His "servants anymore."[91]

Mary is "the mother of His members, which we are: because she cooperated with love, so that the faithful should be born in the **Church,** who are members of His Head."[92] Sixteen centuries later, Thomas Merton described the new-born children of the Mother of Jesus, the 'members of His Head:

"...the 'new being' of the Christian, his [the

Holy Spirit's] 'new creation,' is the effect of an inner *revolution* which in its ultimate and most radical significance implies *complete self-transcendence and transcendence of the norms and attitudes of any given culture, [of] any merely human society. This includes transcendence even of religious practices…. He [the Christian] is henceforth superior to the laws and norms of any religious society, since he is bound by the higher law of love…"*[93]

Merton's assertion that the "new being of the Christian is "superior to the laws and norms of any religious society" coincides with Jesus' words

"I give you a new commandment: love one another; just as I have loved you, you also must love one another. By this love you have for one another, everyone will know that you are my disciples" (*John* 13; 34-35).

From the moment she was conceived, Mary was freed from the old laws and conventions of her religious society. With the Father's grace, Mary was "born again", immaculately conceived, free from any possible spiritual infirmity. Only such a pure human being could be the new Eve, capable of becoming the Virgin Mother of God's son. At the Annunciation she revealed the meaning of this new freedom from sin: putting God's will above her own and above the norms and conventions of Israel.

From the moment Mary said "Let it be done according to thy Word," it was revealed that the law of God is the law of Love. All social conventions – especially the sexual manifestations of Love – are now and forever subject to the higher law of Love:

> "The act of sexual love should by its very nature be joyous, unconstrained, alive, leisurely, inventive, and full of a special delight which the lovers have learned by experience to create for one another. *There is no more beautiful gift of God than the little secret world of creative love and expression in which two persons who have totally surrendered to each other manifest and celebrate their mutual gift. It is precisely in this spirit of celebration, gratitude, and joy that true purity is found.*"[94]

The apostles began to do as Jesus had instructed them even before he disappeared from their midst. Their mission was to "...be my witnesses not only in Jerusalem but throughout Judaea and Samaria, and indeed to the ends of the earth."[95] Jesus' message of Love was and is delivered in male-dominated languages and cultures. [96]

Humanity was and is ruled by power-driven men, as illustrated in a recent newspaper headline: "Sources on women's issues? Men."[97] In another article, "Kate's breasts … our attitude on women's bodies," we find the following lines:

> "The sexual revolution came and went, and yet women are still not as truly sexually free as they deserve to be -- here or around the world. They are not yet, as these struggles show, fully free to define the meanings of their bodies and their desires, to assert their sexual wishes without punishment — including punishment by the state."[98]

The Virgin Mary was aware that her submission to God's will and subsequent pregnancy was an act of rebellion against traditional religious and moral values. Her fiat recalls the attitude of Tancredi,[99] who explained his reasons for joining Garibaldi's forces, instead of remaining loyal to the king: "If we want everything to remain as is, everything must change."[100]

Thanks to Mary, human love underwent a true revolution; with her, through her, and in her, God revealed that He is Love and that Love is omnipotent. Mary's consent to her Lover restored God's eternal kingdom on Earth.[101]

Virgin Mary and Jesus, Persian miniature

## CHAPTER 5

# MARY'S PREGNANCY ANNOUNCES THE NEW LAW

Mohammed claimed that the Almighty had revealed to him the mysteries of Creation. The prophet also claimed Allah had indicated how to govern and control his peoples, executing the *shariah* law.[102] After Mohammed's death, his disciples wrote down

Allah's messages. Allegedly, in the prophet's words, the *Qur'an* was to be the definitive conclusion of the Jewish and Christian scriptures.

Regarding the mother of Jesus, Surah 19 is named *Maryam* after Mary and other surahs echo the New Testament accounts of the Annunciation:

> "And remember when the angels said: 'O Mary! Verily, Allah has chosen you, purified you (from polytheism and disbelief), and chosen you above the women of the Alamin (mankind) of her lifetime." Surah 42. "O Mary! Submit yourself with obedience to your Lord..." Surah 43.

> "Remember when the angels said: 'O Mary! Verily Allah gives you the glad tidings of a Word ['Be' and he was! Jesus the son of Mary] from Him, his name will be the Messiah. Jesus the son of Mary, held in honor in this world and in the hereafter, and will be one of those near to Allah." Surah 45.

> "She said: 'O my Lord! How shall I have a son when no man has touched me?' He said: 'So it will be for Allah creates what He wills. When He has decreed something, He says to it only 'Be!' and it is." Surah 47.

It must be kept in mind that Mohammed was not just the 'prophet' of Islam, but also a political leader who created an earthly kingdom by sheer military power. Islam was and is of this world, ruled by the *Shari'a* law, which binds individuals, society, and the state in all matters.[103] However, Allah's telling of the elevation, purification, and impregnation of Mary did not transform the pagan culture of machismo that still exists in most if not all Islamic nations.[104] Islam is ruled by the *Shari'a*; the Body of Christ by Divine Love.

Those who believe the Virgin's story, from the Annunciation to Pentecost, can still hear her words, "Do whatever he tells you." To satisfy that request the apostles would have to accommodate the power of earthly authorities. From the earliest days of His Church, Christ's apostles confused the authority to rule His Kingdom with the temporal powers and mores found on Earth.[105] "Western Christianity has often been associated with a spiritual-will-power and an instinct for organization and authority."[106]

"You must obey the governing authorities," St. Paul wrote to the Romans, "Since all government comes from God, the civil authorities were appointed by God, and so anyone who resists authority is resisting against God's decision, and such an act is bound to be punished."[107]  St. Paul would lose all his powers as a Roman citizen before entering the Kingdom of God: he was beheaded at the hands of the "God-appointed" civil authorities in the capital of the Empire.

As His apostles spread the good news,[108] Christ's followers heard a compromised version of His message and that of his mother. Both Mother and Son announced the new order of Creation, truly a *Novus ordo seclorum* ruled by the Law of Love. To paraphrase Merton, "*the norms and attitudes of any given culture, [of] any merely human society*" were and are now subject to the order of Love, the New Covenant. Human blood — circumcision and the blood of Christ respectively — is essential to validate the myths of the Old and the New Covenants. Both refer to the man-God/God-man relationship, revealed first in *Genesis* (YHW to Abraham) and later in the Gospels (Jesus to his Church).

> "When Abram was ninety-nine years old Yahweh appeared to him and said, 'I am El Shaddai. Bear yourself blameless in my presence, and I will make a Covenant between myself and you, and increase your numbers greatly.
>
> "Abram bowed to the ground and God said this to him: 'Here now is my covenant with you: *you shall become the father of a multitude of nations… I will establish my Covenant between myself and you…a Covenant in perpetuity…*.

"God said to Abraham, 'You on your part shall maintain my Covenant...generation after generation. Now this is my Covenant which you are to maintain between myself and you, and your descendants after you: all your males must be circumcised. You shall circumcise your foreskin [*a practice believed to increase male fertility*], and this shall be the sign of the Covenant between myself and you.[…] The uncircumcised male, whose foreskin has not been circumcised, such a man shall be cut off from his people: he has violated my Covenant."[109]

In the New Covenant, Jesus offers His own blood "for the forgiveness of sins;" it is the "mystery of faith." C. S. Lewis wrote in *Mere Christianity* that "every other moment from the beginning of the world - is always the Present for Him," including of course, Jesus' Passover supper with His apostles.

God is not in Time, He is always Present in his Creation, and consequently in the Eucharist, the sacrament of the New Covenant:

"He did the same with the cup after supper, and said, 'This cup is the new covenant in my blood which will be poured out for you."[110]

## Christ Perfects Abraham's Covenant

Christ's crucifixion brings the Covenant YHW made with Abraham to perfection, but was Jesus' sacrifice on the cross contradicting His Father's Covenant with Abraham "in perpetuity"? There is no such contradiction: Jesus brings the old Covenant to perfection with his own blood.[111] "It is accomplished; and bowing His head he gave up his spirit."[112] "Later He *breathed* on His apostles: 'Receive the Holy Spirit…'"[113]

St. Paul makes it clear that "Jesus has overridden the Law, and cancelled every record of the debt that we had to pay. He has done away with it [the Law] by nailing it to the cross."[114] YHW had told Abraham "You shall circumcise your foreskin, and this shall be the sign of the Covenant between myself and you." Jesus tells us "By this love you have for one another, everyone will know that you are my disciples."[115]

> "I saw the holy city, the new Jerusalem, coming down out of heaven from God, prepared as a bride beautifully dressed for her husband. And I heard a loud voice from the throne saying, "Now the dwelling of God is with men, and he will live with them. They will be his people, and God

> himself will be with them and …wipe
> every tear from their eyes. There will be no
> more death or mourning or crying or pain,
> for the old order of things has passed away."
> He who was seated on the throne said, 'I
> am making everything new!' Then he
> said, 'write this down, for these words
> are trustworthy and true.' He said to me:
> 'It is done. I am the alpha and the omega,
> the beginning and the end.'"[116]

Jesus brought the Old Covenant to perfection not "in perpetuity" but in eternity. "All the days are 'Now' for Him" (C. S. Lewis, *Mere Christianity*, 148). The Son of God and Mary revealed that both covenants were sealed with blood; circumcision, representing *biological fertility* in the Mosaic Covenant, and Christ's blood, representing the *fertility of Love* in the New Covenant.[117] Both covenants prepare us for our own wedding feast with God:

> "That is why you, my brothers, who
> through the body of Christ are now dead
> to the Law, can now give yourselves to
> another husband, to him who rose from
> the dead *to make us productive for God*. Before our conversion our sinful passions,
> quite unsubdued by the Law, *fertilized our
> bodies* to make them give birth to death.

> But now we are rid of the Law, freed by death of our imprisonment, free to serve in the new spiritual way *and not the old way of a written law.*"[118]

Jesus ("I am the way") is the "new spiritual way." The new Law is revealed at the Annunciation when Love becomes flesh. Mary's fiat means the Bride can now join her Divine Lover and proclaim His love for her:

> "The Bride: Wine flowing straight to my Beloved, As it runs on the lips of those who sleep. I am my Beloved's / and his desire is for me. Come, my Beloved, / let us go into the fields. We will spend the night in the villages, And in the morning we will go to the vineyards. […] Then I shall give you / the gift of my love."[119]

### The Aftermath of Mary's Revolution

The status of human sexuality through millennia of recorded history until our own days can be summarized in Joseph Campbell's words:

> "…as for *eros* (mere biological, physical love), it's really the lure and appeal of the organs to organs – in the dark anyone will do. In the early orgiastic cults, indiscriminate love was the rule; and one doesn't have to go back that far to encounter love of that kind."[120]

"According to Friedrich Nietzsche," wrote Pope Benedict XVI in his first encyclical *Deus Caritas Est,* "Christianity had poisoned *eros*, which for its part, while not completely succumbing, gradually degenerated into vice." The remaining text of the encyclical clarifies the role of *eros* in the Mystical Body of Christ; like *agape*, erotic love is a manifestation of God:

> "it is neither the spirit alone nor the body alone that loves: it is man, the person, a unified creature composed of body and soul, who loves. Only when both dimensions are truly united, does man attain his full stature. Only thus is love —*eros*—able to mature and attain its authentic grandeur."[121]

By virtue of Mary's response to God's messenger, "the lure and appeal of the organs to organs" underwent a complete revolution. With Mary's cooperation, God transformed the "mere biological, physical [manifestation of] love" into an "outward sign of his inward **grace**."[122]

As of the instant in which Mary said, "You see before you the Lord's servant, let it happen to me as you have said," the Spirit of God redefined human procreation to mean the procreation of the Mystical Body of Christ. Popular belief has it that loving mothers know intuitively how their children will behave, act, and even think in their lifetime. Mary's unconditional submission to the Divine Father of her child transfigured her into a sacrament, a sign of His grace.

Jesus learned the New Law from His Virgin Mother, observing her life of total dedication to the Father of her child.[123] The Virgin Mother taught her Son "You shall love the Lord your God with all your heart, and with all your soul, and with all your mind." Mary did not need to hear Jesus' proclamation that "This is the great and first commandment. And a second is like it. You shall love your neighbor as yourself;" Mary knew and obeyed the New Law from the moment of her own immaculate conception.[124]

Once Jesus proclaimed the commandments of the New Covenant, *all* human actions took on a new meaning. "Do whatever he tells you," now meant that the Holy Spirit had revealed to her that it was time for Jesus to manifest the love of His Father for His Blessed Mother. In other words, the Virgin Mother knew intuitively that for the rest of his life on Earth, Jesus would behave, act, and even think in a manner that would revolutionize "all the laws and the prophets."[125]

In the words of Benedict XVI, "True revolution consists in simply turning to God who is the measure of what is right and who at the same time is everlasting love. And what could ever save us apart from love?"[126] And it was Mary who brought Love to the world in the person of her Son.

CHAPTER 6

# THE SACRAMENT OF LOVE, THE NEW LAW

The "outward sign of God's inward grace," God's sacrament, is His Son, who restored God's divine kinship to each human being.[127] From the moment Mary agrees to do God's will, *eros* manifests Love on Earth. Erotic behavior is no longer "pure 'sex'—a commodity, a mere 'thing' to be bought and sold,"[128] it is now transformed into Divine Love. God's grace begets His son; still a virgin, Mary is impregnated by God, the Father. The procreation of Love is not physical but spiritual:

> "Mary said to the angel, 'But how can
> this come about, since I am a virgin?'
> 'The Holy Spirit will come upon you'
> the angel answered, 'and the power of
> the Most High will cover you with his
> shadow.'[129]

The Holy *Spirit*, the power of the Most High, "His shadow," directly impregnates Mary. In this act, the Almighty reveals the *sacred, spiritual* nature of impregnation, pregnancy, and nativity among humans. In Mary's myth, the Father of her son is not her fiancée, not God's messenger, but God Himself. Nothing created, no burning bush, no king, no angel, no creature mediates between God the lover and Mary His beloved nor between Mary the lover and her beloved. Love reproduces itself in the flesh provided by the Virgin's ovum, made fertile by the omnipotent creative Spirit of God the Father.[130]

Through Mary, Love procreates a new Adam: Jesus, the new Israel, His Mystical Body. "Now a great sign appeared in heaven: a woman, [...] She was pregnant, and in labor, crying aloud in the pangs of childbirth."[131] Like Mary, the woman described by Saint John gives birth to the savior of the human race; the Messiah, not from Israel but from God. "The woman brought *a male child into the world,* the son who was *to rule all the nations…*"[132] The mystery underlying Mary's story will never be completely revealed: it is God's myth, not hers.

There are human experiences that constantly reveal the mystery of Love: the exercise of free will is one of them. Humans may reject the eternal Authorship of Love and in so doing, embrace temporal power instead. The antagonistic relation "temporal power/eternal Authority (Love)" is experienced by anyone aware of the love/hate conflict present in all of us.

From Spike Lee's *Do the right thing.*

In *Huis Clos,* a famous play by Jean-Paul Sartre, *"les autres son l'enfer"*:[133] others are Hell, and there is no way out of their infernal company. The only way to escape the Hell of hatred is to "love the Lord your God with all your heart, and with all your soul," and [...to] "love your neighbor as yourself."[134] The antagonism between Jesus and the Tempter is illustrated in St. John's *Revelation*:

> "Then the dragon (Satan) was enraged with the woman and went away to make war on the rest of her children, that is, all who obey God's commandments and bear witness for Jesus."[135]

The "woman" described in St. John's *Book of Revelation* is the mother of the Messiah, the Church, the Mystical Body of Christ, Mary's child.

## Again, on Love

The energy of Creation – Love - and its *modus operandi* on Earth helps us understand Pope Benedict XVI's "true revolution."[136] The revolution of Love initiated by Mary at the moment of the Annunciation was foreseen and foretold among diverse nations in the past.

The Greco-Roman cultural heritage includes the divine character of Love. Five centuries before the Virgin Mary told her story, Socrates had accepted Love as God:

> "As I was saying then, Phaedrus opened with some such arguments as these – that Love was a great god... The worship of this god, he said, is of the oldest, for Love is unbegotten, nor is there mention of his parentage to be found anywhere in either prose or verse.
> [...] Thus we find that the antiquity of Love is universally admitted, and in very truth he is the ancient source of all our highest good. [...] And again, nothing but Love will make a man offer his life for another's..."[137]

Socrates explained the energy of Love as the omnipotent force of creation, that which constitutes the "highest good" of humanity. Like Israel's YHW, Socrates' Love is the Creator of all there is: the Athenian sage quotes the poet Hesiod:

> "From Chaos rose broad-bosomed Earth, the sure / And everlasting seat of all that is, / And after, Love…"[138]

In the *Symposium*, Plato reveals essential characteristics of Love as it is manifested among humans. Although the dialogue concentrates on *eros*, "only philosophy can know truly the role of the god Dionysus, *the communication of divine life to men, and this as mediated through eros.*"[139] Love creates and divinizes man: "Love can light the beacon which man must steer by when he sets out to live the better life."[140]

Dante Alighieri left us a beautiful description of Love and of its relationship with each of us. With a total mastery of St. Thomas Aquinas' theology, the great Florentine Christianized Aristotle and the neo-Platonists. In his *Commedia* (Giovanni Boccaccio added *Divina* to this title):

> "The experience of love becomes a means to self-realization, and an awareness of the hierarchy of forces operative in the universe at large, which makes possible an

> *ascensus mentis ad sapientiam*, to that *amoroso*
> *uso della sapienza* which enables the human
> mind to participate in the divine." [141]

Half a century after Dante's death (1321), Boccaccio completed his *Esposizioni sopra la Commedia di Dante* (1374), high praise for his fellow Florentine from one of the most renowned intellectuals of the Italian Renaissance. Boccaccio's treatment of erotic love, however, was different from Dante's as can be gleaned from the following lines:

> "And if, perchance, they do, after all,
> contain here and there a trifling indis-
> cretion of speech, such as might ill sort
> with one of your precious prudes, who
> weigh words rather than deeds, and are
> more concerned to appear, than to be,
> good, I say that so to write was as per-
> missible to me, as 'tis to men and wom-
> en at large in their converse to make use
> of such terms as …"[142]

Yet, Boccaccio's sensual stories do honor the presence of the Divinity in all loves: "Wherefore, it but remains for me to render, *first to God*, and then to you, my thanks, and so to give a rest to my pen and weary hand."[143]

Dante's understanding of the apostle John's affirmation that "God is Love"[144] affirmation is beautifully expressed in the concluding lines of his *Commedia*:

> "Exalted fantasy at this point was lacking power; but my desire and my will were already turning, just like a wheel that is equally moved, by the Love that moves the sun and the other stars."[145]

It is interesting to note how Dante makes the end (omega) of his *Paradise* in stanza #33 coincide with its beginning (alpha) in Canto 1:

> "The glory of Him who moves every thing penetrates through the universe, and shines  more in one part and less in another."[146]

By equating A and Ω, the poet reminds us that Love moves everything in Creation, God is present from beginning to end: "I am the Alpha and the Omega, the First and the Last, the Beginning and the End."[147]

Half a century before Benedict XVI's *Deus Caritas Est*, Denis de Rougemont wrote a most penetrating insight into the energy of Creation — Love — and its *modus operandi* on Earth.[148] Frequently, Pope Benedict echoes de Rougemont's essay:

> "Two things emerge clearly from this rapid overview of the concept of *eros* past and present. First, there is a certain relationship

between love and the Divine: love promises infinity, eternity—a reality far greater and totally other than our everyday existence. Yet we have also seen that the way to attain this goal is not simply by submitting to instinct. Purification and growth in maturity are called for; and these also pass through the path of renunciation. Far from rejecting or "poisoning" *eros*, they heal it and restore its true grandeur. This is due first and foremost to the fact that man is a being made up of body and soul. Man is truly himself when his body and soul are intimately united; the challenge of *eros* can be said to be truly overcome when this unification is achieved;" [149] and, "The erotic process introduces into life an element foreign to […] sexual attraction—a desire that never relapses, that nothing can satisfy, that even rejects and flees the temptation to obtain fulfillment in the world, because its demand is to embrace no less than the All (sic). It is *infinite transcendence*, man's rise into his god. And this rise is *without return*." [150]

The Spanish thinker José Ortega y Gasset also wrote on love, in 'studies' t h a t reflect views similar to those of Pope Ratzinger and de Rougemont. These men wrote that "[love] is *infinite* transcendence, man's rise into his god," (de Rougemont) and that "love promises infinity, eternity — a reality far greater and totally other than our everyday existence" (Pope Benedict XVI). One particular text of Ortega y Gasset approximates both the German and the French authors:

> "To love something is to be committed to its existence [...] But note that this is the same as continuously giving life to it [...] To love is perennial life-giving, creation, and intentional conservation of the beloved."[151]

All poets, writers, philosophers, and theologians inspired by Love become its instruments:

> "Not by art, then, they make their poetry ... but by *divine dispensation...God himself is the speaker*, and through them he shows he shows his meaning to us."[152]

Two millennia have passed since the Virgin Mary revealed the identity of the divine "speaker:" His Word became her flesh. Yet, many do not listen.

### The True Revolution: That of Love

The revolution that Christ accomplished at Golgotha put an end to the old order that had existed in

Israel. The son of the Virgin Mary instituted a New Covenant to restore humanity to its original perfection; His was a revolution of love. His words at the Last Supper transformed the Passover Seder into the sacrament of the New Covenant.

All four evangelists and Saint Paul describe the institution of the ultimate symbol of God's love for humanity, the Eucharist.[153] Jesus is the perfect sacrificial gift to God: "Father, into your hands I commit my spirit.' With these words he breathed his last."[154] The Virgin Mary's revolution was complete: Love had become one of us, a mortal human. The Father's love engendered a new Adam, his son Jesus, thanks to the Virgin Mary's consent.

As Pope Benedict puts it:

"There is one more important point in the Gospel account of the Annunciation which should be underlined, one which never fails to strike us: God asks for our "yes"; He has created a free partner in dialogue [the Mystical Body of His Son], from whom He requests a reply in complete liberty. God asks for Mary's free consent that He may become man. To be sure, the "yes" of the Virgin is the fruit of divine grace, but grace does not eliminate freedom; on the contrary it creates and sustains it. Faith removes nothing from the human creature, rather it permits his full and final realization."[155]

# PART III

# LOVE/*EROS* RESTORED

Part III of *The Virgin Mary's Revolution*, "Love/*Eros* restored,"[156] further reveals the essence of erotic Love to those who believe Mary's story. What was stated in the opening chapters of this work, i.e. that the true revolution of human sexuality began with the Virgin Mary's consent to God, is confirmed by our own experience of the Divine life. Finally, the testimonials of persons who have witnessed Love's Creative Presence rebut the evil of malicious rumors  we saw in the opening chapter.

## CHAPTER 1

# THE ETERNAL PRESENCE OF DIVINE LOVE/*EROS* IN HUMAN NATURE

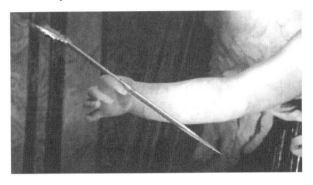

Bernini, Ecstasy of Saint Therese,detail

The presence of Love in each human being is demonstrated by even the most casual introspection of anyone's acts. Consciously or not, these acts are meant to benefit their agent. This benevolence is itself a sign of Love. Arguments *ex autoritate principis* serve little purpose here: the reader will find various bibliographical references that confirm the basic tenets of this chapter. Is the Law of Love found in the Old Covenant? Did the Virgin Mary need to hear or know the lessons of the Old Testament to accept what God requested of her? Why was she willing to reject her own Jewish traditions and laws to accept God's message at the Annunciation?

## The Law of Moses and the Law of Love

The Law of Love is both implicit and explicit in the Old Covenant. It is God who establishes the terms of our relationship to Him;[157] and it is He who revealed his Law to Moses.[158] Absent, how-ever, was the full revelation of the Law of Love; that would happen "when the appointed time came."[159] The angel Gabriel announced the "fullness of time" to Mary, telling her, "you are to conceive and bear son, and you must name him Jesus." Her fiancé Joseph was also informed of the pregnancy of his wife-to-be in a dream: *"The virgin will conceive and ive birth to a son and they will call him Emmanuel,"* which means 'God-is-with-us.'"

Love became flesh in Mary's womb: her son is now one of us, visible and historic.[160] Eternally historic, which means God is omnipresent, present at all times and in all places. Love is present at the cre ation of time, present in time, and present at the end of time. Love is the Alpha/Omega of Creation.[161]

The full revelation of Love/*eros* occurs in the "fullness of time." The Law of Love is revealed not only in the Old Testament, but whenever and wherever Love is present.

## The Virgin Mary's Divine Lover

The central question in the second part of this book, "Did the Virgin Mary need to hear or know the lessons of the Old Testament to assent to God's request?" is answered by her own question: "But how can this come about, since I have no knowledge of man?" She was in fact rebelling against the Law of Moses by accepting her Divine Lover's proposition. The Virgin Mary had no need to hear or know the Mosaic Law to suffer the consequences of becoming pregnant by someone other than Joseph. "God's favor" gave her the courage to obey her Divine Lover, but that courage did not justify her actions in the eyes of her elders nor the Jewish authorities.

Years later, guided by the Spirit of her son, the early Fathers of the Church believed that the Virgin Mary had been immaculately conceived and from that instant she was full of God's grace.[162]

## Influences on Christian Sexuality

As indicated earlier, "Throughout humanities' history many institutions and religions have spread mistaken concepts about our sexuality." Those erroneous teachings respond to earthly concerns rather than to the eternally true nature of our sexuality as revealed to the Virgin Mary.

From her beginning at Pentecost, the Church adopted the cultures and traditions of different peoples to spread the Good News of Jesus' message. The process of acculturation among the Apostles was initiated in Greek.[163] This language *informed, transformed, and conformed* the message of Jesus to humanity. "What makes the Church catholic is the fact that Christ in His saving mission embraces all humanity [...] the true character of His Messianism: a mission directed to the whole man and to every man."[164]

"*Logos*," "catholic," Eucharist, and "martyr" are Greek words used to express concepts and beliefs that are essential to Christianity. To *inform* the nations of the world about the Heavenly Jerusalem, the apostles used Greek, including its intellecttual rules and cultural structures. The nononsense parables and the straightforward message of Jesus were *transformed* by a philosophical vocabulary to *conform* it to *this* world and not necessarily to the Kingdom of God. The sacrament of the Eucharist provides an excellent example of this linguistic acculturation. The mystery behind the words, "This is my body," is allegedly *explained* in our day as "a bond of unity… a real foundation for the covenant between God and man."[165]

From the beginning of the Church, eating "the body and blood of Jesus Christ" was translated into the Greek εὐ χαριστια (*eucharistia* or "thanksgiving"). This term belies the transcendental miracle of the event that enables humanity to be reunited to the Father. Only in solidarity with His Son can we—like the prodigal son—be reinstated to the divine status of "sons of God."

Another example of our Babel-like attitude regarding the Eucharist is found in the Catechism, a publication "offered to *all* the faithful."[166] There we find the following terms referring to the mystery of Jesus' words, "This is my body:"

> "The Eucharist is the efficacious sign
> and sublime cause of that communion
> in the divine life and that unity of the
> People of God."[167]

Catechism #1328-1332 try to express "the inexhaustible richness of this sacrament" using various names, including the Greek words *eucharistein* and *eulogein,* recalling the Jewish blessings.[168]

Jesus' message of Love necessarily implies acculturation since it is addressed to all human beings. The Eternal Word became flesh in a specific culture but, throughout history, God made His covenants with humanity at large. God expressed Himself in His Creation; that is His "language," it needs no translation.[169] Who would pretend to explain God's Word — His Creation — in mere words?

> "Ever since God created the world his eternal power and divine nature – however invisible – have been there for the mind to see in the things He has made, so that men are without excuse (*Romans* 1:20)."[170]

## Greek and Jewish Influences

Both Greek and Jewish cultures — as well as many found in other ancient civilizations — were and are laden with negative and misogynist views and attitudes regarding sexuality. To spread the Good News of Jesus, the Apostles had to adopt the Greek language and adapt their message to the religious traditions with which they were familiar. The influence of those traditions has prevailed through the ages to our own days.

Yale professor of Christian Ethics, Dr. Margaret A. Farley, describes the Greek influence this way:

"The tensions in the Jewish tradition from the beginning, between its affirmative attitude toward sex and its concern for the dangers of the sexual impulse, grew sharply when Jewish thinkers were influenced by Hellenistic philosophers."[171]

Eros,
Cycladic Art museum,
Athens

**Modigliani,** *Red Nude*

Dr. Farley goes on to explain how contemporary Judaism, "like other religious communities," has not resolved the age-old tensions in their views of human sexuality, "in particular, those of women and of gay men and lesbians."[172] "Freud's Jewishness was essentially opposed to biblical law and to the rabbinic tradition which expounded the law. For Freud, that Law leads to guilt and guilt precipitates neuroses."[173]

Christ's disciples and their followers failed to heed the Virgin Mary's advice to the servers at the wedding feast of Cana, "Do whatever he tells you." Nor did they follow her example in rejecting the Mosaic laws.[174] Whereas the blood of circumcision had sealed the Old Covenant, Mary's Son proclaimed the New Law of Love and sealed it with His blood: "This cup is the new testament in my blood, which is shed for you."[175]

> "If you want to be perfect, go, sell what you have and give to the poor, and you will have treasure in heaven; and come, follow Me:"[176]

The Apostles followed Jesus, but they held on to the Mosaic laws. Their adherence to the rules and regulations concerning sexual behavior is one salient example. Even after the Council in Jerusalem, when the Apostles agreed to forego the Mosaic Laws for Gentiles entering the Church, they held on to many traditional social and political regulations (dietary rules, laws on fornication, and idolatry).

For example, in his *Letter*, St. Jude adheres primarily to the Mosaic and Natural Laws rather that to that proclaimed by Jesus. Specifically referring to "The fornication of Sodom and Gomorrah" (*Jude*, 7), the writer warns of "eternal fire," a form of divine punishment found throughout the Old Testament.

Only after 20 verses (out of 25) in which he refers no fewer than 8 times to the Old Testament, St. Jude dedicates the last five to the lessons he might have learned from Jesus' words and examples:

> "Keep yourselves within the love of God
> and wait for the mercy of our Lord Jesus
> Christ to give you eternal life" (*Jude,* 21).

Two thousand years later, the sexual mores of Christians are still regulated by laws and criteria of the Old Covenant, which had become obsolete as of the instant the Virgin Mary became pregnant "outside" of marriage.[177] Cooperating intimately with the Virgin Mary, God revealed the supernatural dimension of human sexuality at the Annunciation.

Millions of years of biological evolution resulted in complementary sexuality for the purpose of reproduction among humans and other forms of life.

Two characteristics essential to the *specifically human sexuality* condition are *intelligence* and *free will*.

Those two characteristics were, are, and will be possible because the Spirit of the Creator included them in the Evolutionary Process. *All* inclusions imply a decision; they are not chance occurrences. Free from any doubt or emotional barriers, with a pure heart,[178] the Virgin Mary saw through (*intus-legit*) her own amazement. She accepted *willingly* her Lover's invitation to procreate Love in her body.

Billions of years after Creation, the true nature of human sexuality was revealed; the reproduction of Love on Earth.[179] The *supernatural* reason for complementary sexuality among humans transcended the mere biological ends defined by Darwinian evolution. At the Annunciation, the Divine Lover revealed to Mary and thorough her to the Body of her Son, that the reproduction of Himself superseded the reproduction of human beings.[180] Sex, like all human actions, has no other reason than to project God's Love in his Creation *eternally*:[181] the reproduction of *temporal* physical "images" of human parents, "the procreation of children is not essential to marriage."[182] The "complementariness" of human sexuality is no longer a biological necessity of mankind but rather an essential *spiritual* condition to manifest Love on Earth.[183]

After the Virgin Mary's revolutionary act (doing God's will), human sexuality became a supernatural symbol of Love/*eros*. God's messenger tells her she is "full of grace;" she is like a sacrament as defined by her Son:

> "I give you a new commandment: love one another; just as I have loved you, you also must love one another. By this love you have for one another, everyone will know that you are my disciples."[184]

## Other Religious Influences on Christian Sexuality: The Kama Sutra

A cursory analysis of passages from other religious scriptures confirms the fact that "Throughout the history of humanity many institutions and religions have spread mistaken and therefore detrimental concepts about our sexuality."

The writing of the *Kama Sutra* coincides approximately with the translation of the Hebrew Bible into Greek circa 250 BCE known as the Septuagint. Most scholars agree with Indra Singha that

> The *Kama Sutra* is not just an exclusive sex manual; it presents itself as a guide to a virtuous and gracious living that discusses the nature of love, family life and other aspects pertaining to pleasure-

oriented    faculties    of    human
life."[185]

However, this ancient scripture does not transcend human sense experiences nor does it pretend to reach the spiritual dimension of the nature of love:

> "The basic definition of Kama is the special contact between the sensory organ
> and its object, and the resulting pleasure
> is known as Kama. Kama is taught by the
> Kama Sutras (verses of desire) and by experience."[186]

In the cultural evolution of human sexuality an ideological line  can be traced from the *Kama Sutra* to the Epicureans to Utilitarianism, ending, in the latter half of the twentieth century, in the writings of Joseph Campbell and Hugh Heffner:

> "...as for *eros* (mere biological, physical love), it's really the lure and appeal of the organs to organs..."[187]

Clearly, none of those ideologies relate to the Virgin Mary's intimate experience of Love. In the *Kama Sutra*, Vatsyayana defines *Kama* as one of three necessities for happiness on Earth; the others are *Dharma* and *Artha*. All three explain how humans must live in order to secure a perfectly balanced existence. Men must obey the Holy Scriptures performing designated rituals and sacrifices (Dharma); they must acquire wealth (Artha), and thirdly, humans must enjoy sensual pleasures through the five biological senses (Kama).

## Islam

For Muslims ("those who submit to God"), erotic love is not a human manifestation of God. It is a manifestation of human nature and may be a means of cooperating with Allah's plan in  propagating the species:  "Above all else Islam is naturalism and Islamic spirituality is the plenitude of Nature."[188]

Islamic culture presents a more complicated version of human sexuality, its meaning, and its manifestations. This is due to a number of factors, such as the fact that the various religious "denominations"of Islam cannot be separated from the political entities included in that name. More than a religious faith, Muhammad established a nation, Islam:

> "Muhammad conquered his promised land, and during his lifetime achieved victory and power in this world, exercising political as well as prophetic authority. As the Apostle of God, he brought and taught a religious revelation. But at the same time, as the head of the Muslim *Umma*, he promulgated laws, dispensed

justice, collected taxes, conducted diplomacy, and made peace. The *Umma*, which began as a community, had become a state. It would soon become an empire."[189]

Immediately after the death of Muhammad, Islam, the religion and its juridical structure underwent divisions derived from its military and geopolitical origins:

"People read, understand, and interpret their sources of sacred meaning in relation to the hopes and fears that define their daily lives. *It is therefore not always possible to talk of one Islamic reality*, and less so of one Shia or one Sunni reality. Piety and politics for Shias and Sunnis alike are shaped by the particularities of life in societies as varied as those of India, Iran, and Saudi Arabia."[190]

Islamic sexual mores vary according to the culture of each Muslim tribe or nation, but one characteristic is common to all of them — sexual customs are definitely male-centric:

"Men are the protectors and maintainers of women, because Allah has made one of them to excel the other, and because they spend (to support them) from their means. Therefore the righteous women

are devoutly obedient (to Allah and to
their husbands), and guard in the husband's absence what Allah orders them to
guard (e.g. their chastity, their husband's
property)...."[191]

According to the Qur'an, human sexuality is, with God's efficient cooperation, a means of procreation. Allah endowed sexual acts with carnal pleasures which are not to be rejected without disobeying Him. According to the Qur'an, Muhammad himself was reprimanded by Allah when he chose not to have sex with any of his nine wives:

"O Prophet! Why do you forbid for yourself that which Allah has allowed to you,
seeking to please your wives?"[192]

### Is Love/*Eros* Truly Omnipresent?

The restoration of Love/*eros* in our daily lives entails no contradiction to either the Law of Moses, the Old Covenant, or to natural law. Jesus proclaims the New Covenant, subsumes the Old into his New Law, and asks his disciples to spread the Good News throughout the World. Jesus' Father reveals the New Covenant — His Son — directly to the Virgin Mary. The New Law consists of one thing: doing God's will above all things.

However, there have been and continue to be, persons and institutions that spread misinformation that negates Jesus' message as it refers to our sexuality. One reason to reject the New Law of Love is that it liberated us from rules and regulations that conveniently reduced our moral and social obligations to obeying them and performing mechanical rituals.

One more question comes to mind: does the Virgin Mary's *revolution* affect *all* men and women, or only those who adhere to the Old Covenant? Did she, in rejecting the Laws of Moses, announce the *restoration* of Creation to her Divine Lover?

Is Love/*Eros* present in *all* human beings or only in those born heterosexual? According to Pope Benedict XVI's encyclical *Deus caritas est*, the question is absurd if asked within the context of Jesus' commandments:

> "It is characteristic of mature love that it calls into play all man's potentialities; it engages the whole man, so to speak. Contact with the visible manifestations of God's love can awaken within us a feeling of joy born of the experience of being loved. But this encounter also engages our will and our intellect."[193]

Mature erotic Love calls into play *all* of man's potentialities. "It engages the whole man," which means both heterosexual and homosexual human beings. Articles 2357, 2358, and 2359 of the *Catechism of the Catholic Church* address the issue of homosexuality appealing to only one passage in *Genesis* and quoting St. Paul twice. Interestingly, all three quotes refer to the Law of Moses which no longer applies to "the sound teaching that goes with the Good News of the glory of the blessed God, the gospel that was entrusted to me."[194]

In the Old Testament homosexual acts are considered opposed to the natural law and declared abominations. In recent times, some scientists and political activists have concluded that homosexual acts are no more *contra naturam* than those of heterosexuals.[195] Others analyze the issue of homosexuality according to the Mosaic Laws and to a definition of natural law that predates Galileo:

> "Some sexual acts *contra naturam*, such as rape, incest, and the molestation of children and minors, are still criminalized. But the fact that some acts that formerly were considered *contra naturam* have been pronounced legal in the twentieth century does not mean that they are in accord with the natural law. Could 3 percent of the population, because of dif-

> fering sexual attractions, be exceptions to
> the precept of the natural law relating sex
> and procreation?"[196]

Do we believe Benedict XVI when he states that "Contact with the visible manifestations of God's love can awaken within us a feeling of joy born of the experience of being loved?" Are "visible manifestations of God's love" a matter of "sexual attractions?" Can we limit the "visible manifestations" of human love to heterosexual love? Did the Virgin Mary act *contra naturam*? Does "Contact with the visible manifestations of God's love... awaken within us a feeling of joy born of the experience of being loved," even if it is a visible *homosexual* manifestation?

In his early research, renowned psychiatrist Robert Spitzer had concluded that homosexuality was a matter of choice. [197] Somewhat sarcastically, in his 2011 book on the subject, Howard Kainz asked:

> "Could 3 percent of the population, because of differing sexual attractions, be exceptions to the precept of the natural law relating sex and procreation?"[198]

It should be mentioned that Spitzer was influenced by his Jewish cultural heritage and that in 2012 "the most influential psychiatrist of the twentieth century" apologized to the homosexual commu nity for his erroneous conclusions.

Jesuit theologian Joseph Fuchs did not retract his views about Love and humans, although many of them were rejected by Pope Paul VI in the encyclic *Humanae Vitae*. Fuchs writes:

> "In the same way as *love* – when it is gen- uine – does not proclaim a unique de- mand over and above all norms and laws, likewise the *conscience*. It is true that the conscience is the final arbiter for every moral decision; it is also true that man's morality – which is indeed within him – depends on the fidelity of this moral deci- sion to the response of the conscience."[199]

Clearly, Father Fuchs was writing about genuine love, not about laws and regulations.

Josef Fuchs S.J.
(1912–2005)

The final arbiter is not external to us, it is found within each human being.

Kaintz concludes that "the fact that some acts that formerly were considered *contra naturam* have been pronounced legal in the twentieth century does not mean that they are in accord with the natural law."[200]

By contrast, Fuchs reached a conclusion that has little to do with civil legality and everything to do with the presence of Love/*eros* among men:

> "The natural law is (however inadequately) the subject in which love manifests itself and acts. It is the mosaic in whose colorful variety love tries to find its expression. The love of the justified walks only the paths of God whom it loves. *The meaning of the natural law is love. ...* Nevertheless this love is not any human love of God (*amor*) but the love that God himself 'infuses' into the heart of man..."[201]

Thus, the question, "Is Love *Truly* Omnipresent?" must be answered in the affirmative:

> "Yet *eros* and *agape*—ascending love and descending love—can never be completely separated. The more the two, in their different aspects, find a proper unity in the one reality of love, the more the true nature of love in general is realized."[202]

The *Catechism* states that "homosexual persons are called to chastity," a virtue to which heterosexual persons are equally called.[203] A life of virtue and of union with God "engages our will and our intellect," as Benedict XVI wrote; these are the instruments of our soul, not of our bodies:

> "What the Spirit brings is very different: love, joy, peace, patience, kindness, goodness, trustfulness, gentleness and self-control. There can be no law against things like that, of course. You cannot belong to Christ Jesus unless you crucify all self-indulgent passions and desires."[204]

The omnipotent Spirit of God impregnated the Virgin Mother of Jesus. The myth is that her sexuality had no part in that miraculous gestation. Thirty years later, from the unlikeliest place and at the unlikeliest moment, the same Creative Spirit of God engendered Mary's other sons and daughters. "Woman, behold Your Son."[205]

From the moment those words were spoken, we were God's children, restored to His Kingdom. Woman, behold Your Son."[206] Words from a dying man, spoken *in* and *for* eternity, endowed *humanity* with a new identity, that of the Mystical Body of Christ: "For *whoever does the will of My Father who is in heaven, he is my brother and sister....*" [207]

That new *essential* identity results from the Love that creates and unites us,[208] not from our gender, ethnicity, or any other existential characteristics that may describe but do not define who we are. Cases like Mary Magdalene, the woman at the well, the parable of the prodigal son, and others, clearly indicate that Jesus dealt in a completely different manner with those of us who have transgressed against the sexual mores of our day. Contrary to Ortega y Gasset's famous dictum, *"I am NOT I and my circumstances."*[209] The "new Adam" is free from his past and from his sins.

Our real identity, who we *are* – not who we were or will be – comes from the omnipresent, omnipotent Spirit of all that is. Another explanation of the presence of Divine Love/*eros* in human nature was expressed by Pierre Teilhard de Chardin:

> "Considered in its full biological reality, love—that is to say, *the affinity of being with being*—is not peculiar to man.… If there were no real internal propensity to unite, even at a prodigiously rudimentary level—indeed in the molecule itself—it would be physically impossible for love to appear higher up, *with us, in 'hominised' form*. By rights, *to be certain of its presence in ourselves,* we should assume its presence,

at least in an inchoate form, *in everything that is*."[210]

*All* human beings can and ought to manifest Mature Erotic Love, but:

> "An intoxicated and undisciplined *eros*, then, is not an ascent in "ecstasy" towards the Divine, but a fall, a degradation of man. Evidently, *eros* needs to be disciplined and purified if it is to provide not just fleeting pleasure, but a certain foretaste of the pinnacle of our existence, of that beatitude for which our whole being yearns."[211]

To "be perfect, even as your Father in heaven is perfect,"[212] and thus attain eternal happiness, homosexual, heterosexual, bisexual—in short—*all* human beings must exercise "the virtues of self-mastery"[213] whenever they manifest Love/*eros* in their lives, for "Whoever wants to eliminate love is preparing to eliminate man as such."[214]

Self-mastery teaches "them inner freedom, at times by the support of disinterested friendship, by prayer and sacramental grace, they can and should gradually and resolutely approach Christian perfection." [215]

"The visible manifestations of God's love" have no limits.[216] Aesthetically and culturally we may be repelled by some of those manifestations and at tracted by others, but, unless they are clearly and deliberately idolatrous, i.e. *not according to Jesus' commandment of love*, we are not to pass judgment on them.[217] Such judgments are made by Jesus himself, as He did in a number of cases during his life on Earth.[218] Acts "contrary to the natural law" are not the exclusive domain of any one group of human beings, homosexuals, heterosexuals, or bisexuals.

Unworthy as each of us may be, natural law and Darwinian evolution prepare us to be witnesses of our supernatural identities. God's Word made flesh in Mary's womb united us to our Divine Father: "It is love that makes the human person the authentic image of God.[219]

## Love/E*ros* in A*ll* Humans

Erotic Love means quite a different thing from what is understood outside the Virgin Mary's family. The myth stipulates that her "immediate family" comprehends humanity at large. If we are to follow her instructions at the wedding feast of Cana to "do whatever He tells you," no one should be excluded from being in Love. Love and its human manifestation, *eros*, literally animates *all* humans, all creatures.[220]

Profane literature[221], ancient and contemporary philosophers, and most sacred scriptures, witness to the presence of Love/*eros* in Creation and in their authors.[222] The Virgin Mary is the prime example among all such witnesses. In her story, Love/*eros* Himself[223] sets her myth apart from those of all other cultures by giving His Word to live among us.[224]

## CHAPTER 2
# THE FAMILY UNDER
# THE LAW OF LOVE

Piero della Francesca,
*Madonna del Parto*
(detail)

How did the Virgin Mary's *fiat* change the family? The answer requires a basic acquaintance with that institution as she may have known it. Don Feder's assertion that "the traditional (or natural) family is a Jewish invention," is entirely correct only if we accept the *Genesis* myth as history instead of

Divine revelation.[225] Even if we could trace the family back to the creation of Adam and Eve, we would have to credit other Indo-European sources for what today is called "the traditional (or natural) family."

The definitive historical analysis on the origins of the family was published in 1864 by Numa Fustel de Coulanges, *La Cité antique, A Study of the Religion, Law, and Institutions of Greece and Rome.*[226] Fustel de Coulanges concentrated his research on India, Greece, and Rome. The latter two became empires.

Fustel de Coulanges does not include the Law of Moses in his study, and yet, we read in it how the God of Abraham helped establish "the right of property." Yahweh, "the primitive proprietor, by right of creation, delegates to man his ownership over a part of the soil."[227]

De Coulanges also describes basic characteristics of the family, of marriage, and of the role of sexuality at the time of the Annunciation:

1) Domestic religion was the foundation of the family structure in ancient times;

2) The family was a *religious* association and not a natural one;

3) Marriage for the maiden meant abandonment of paternal religion and submission to her husband's house gods;

4) Marriage was obligatory as a safeguard to protect the continuity of the paternal worship;

5) Celibacy was an act of impiety against the family religion;

6) The son perpetuating domestic worship could not sacrifice at two hearths or honor two different lines of ancestors;

7) Upon establishing a new homestead, (*domus*) a man would abandon his father's religion;

8) "Worship of the sacred fire and of ancestors," was transmitted from male to male. It was the sacred duty of the male heirs alone to keep the family worship alive.

These characteristics would vary from region to region under Roman occupation. Judea, for example, was very different from Galilee, her neighbor to the North. In Judea, Jerusalem was the seat of Roman and Jewish power. On the other hand, Galileans were considered an inferior people. They were "hicks" whose lax religious practices, Aramaic language, and lack of sophistication would have made it difficult to take them seriously or respectfully.[228]

When the Virgin Mary consented to do the will of her Divine Lover, she was acting against her religion and local traditions: who would believe her story? The Law of Moses was absolutely clear: to reject parental religion was equivalent to breaking at least two commandments: "Thou shall have no other gods before me," and, "Honor thy father and thy mother."

If indeed marriage was considered obligatory and celibacy impious, the Virgin Mary had already violated those two customs at the moment of the Annunciation.[229] The insistence of some of the Early Christian Fathers regarding Mary's virginity may seem extreme to nonbelievers. There are many reasons for misunderstanding the Virgin Mary's story, but they share in common the ignorance of what it is that we call a "mystery" and the concurrent phenomena, "miracles."

This ignorance may well be deliberate and therefore intractable, or it may be involuntary, in which case true information may eliminate it. St. Augustine wrote a thorough analysis of the profound reasons that justified Mary's virginity:

> "For it behooved that our Head, thanks to a notable miracle, should be born in the flesh of a virgin. This way He was telling us that [we] his members would be *born according to the Spirit* into the virgin Church. Therefore Mary alone is mother and virgin both in the Spirit [of the Church] and in flesh [of Christ]..."[230]

At her young age, Mary had acted against the traditions and regulations of the Old Covenant[231] by choosing a celibate life albeit dedicated to God[232]. St. Augustine affirms that Mary's query, "How can this be since I know no man?" indicates that she had consecrated her virginity as an act of love to God *before* the Annunciation.[233]

In ancient societies, the duties of the family worship and the laws of inheritance applied only to the males: women were not allowed to inherit or to conduct the rites of worship. Thus, both Matthew and Luke trace Jesus' genealogy from Joseph to Adam from male to male. Joseph, Mary's husband-to-be, did not belong to that royal lineage prophesied for Jesus. Was Mary genetically or otherwise connected to kings of Israel, like David and Solomon?

The answer to this question is not found in the New Testament or in the Qur'an. Not even her parents' names are known. The perennial predominance of the males came to a halt with the Virgin Mary. Her story has it that the religious duties and the laws of the Old Covenant had "passed" to the Father of her child, God.

At the risk of her life, the Virgin Mary established a new social order. She liberated the institutions of marriage and the family from the old conventions and regulations. For Mary, "The fear of Yahweh is" NOT "the beginning of wisdom;"[234] doing His will is. In fact, the Father of her child founds an altogether *new* family, according to His own Spirit and not according to the flesh. God and Mary revolutionize the entire universe and *restore* the preternatural order of Creation.[235] The Virgin Mary's revolution produced changes in the evolutionary process of Creation which came to be known as God's ultimate revelation, Jesus. God's word – *Logos* – became a human being.

*The Virgin Mary's "marriage" to God the Father begat a family the likes of which had been known only in the original order of His Creation.*[236] The Virgin Mary was, in Aristotelian jargon, the efficient cause of the new institutions of marriage and family, and in biblical terms, she was the new Eve, the mother of the new Adam.

1) The characteristics enumerated by Fustel de Coulanges and those found in the Mosaic Laws were changed forever:

2) Loving God above all things, i.e. doing the Father's will, makes us His family and not physical or genetic factors;

3) The religion of the homestead – the *domus* – was no longer valid since it was revealed that "home" is that of our Divine Father;

4) The family remains a religious association but liberated from the material rituals of the past;

5) Worship is no longer the sole responsibility of the males in a family. After the Annunciation, worship is conducted by the Virgin Mary, her family, and even female friends and acquaintances;

6) Celibacy, virginity, marriage, and sexuality in general are vali -

dated by the Virgin Mary's impregnation outside "traditional" marriage;

a) Both sons and daughters are bound by the Law of Love and no other;

b) There is only one worship, Love, as revealed by the Father to Mary through their Son;

c) Gender politics in marriage, religion, and sexuality came to an end with the Virgin Mary; she gave birth to a new "Jerusalem," the Body of her son, the Church.

The Virgin Mary's revolution continues in our own days: **we are now *free and* obligated to love.**

These words from the last chapter of *The Ancient City* summarize some of the consequences that resulted from the Virgin Mary's revolution:

"Christianity coming after all this progress in thought and institutions, presented to the adoration of all men a single God, a universal God, a God who belonged to all, who had no chosen people, and who made no distinction in races, families, or states.[237]"

And, a God who makes no distinction based on gender, age, sexuality, political or economic status; "there are no more distinctions between Jew and Greek, slave and free, male and female, but all of you are one in Christ Jesus."[238]

CHAPTER 3

# THE MEASURE OF HUMAN LOVE

Four dimensions of the single reality that is Love: Life, Pleasure, Suffering, and Death:[239]

> "Fundamentally, 'love' is a single reality, but with different dimensions; at different times, one or other dimensions may emerge more clearly."[240]

Even death "can awaken within us a feeling of joy born of the experience of being loved." When Jesus expired on the Cross, we are told, he "gave up his spirit." That same spirit "opens our eyes and allows us to know all reality beyond the limited horizons of individualism and subjectivism which distort our awareness."[241]

Pope Benedict XVI paraphrases the ancient antithetical definitions of reality by Heraclitus and Parmenides when he states that "one or other dimensions may emerge more clearly" at different times from that "single reality" called Love.

Although "*eros* is rooted in man's nature,"[242] manifestations of God's Love/*eros* include acts that may transcend and occasionally transgress the natural laws. We call such acts either "miracles" or "sins," depending on the cultural traditions and morals of the agents.

Miracles or sins, all derive their value from the agents' relation to the Spirit that creates and animates them. The myth we have been considering, the Virgin Mary's pregnancy, reveals one such Divine act. Only God, the Second Person[243], can alter his own creation. Alterations of natural processes are temporal phenomena that reveal the One eternal "single reality"mentioned in Benedict XVI's *Deus Caritas Est*. Thus, the Annunciation, the raising of Lazarus, the transubstantiation of bread and wine, Jesus' resurrection and his many other miracles, reveal "God as Love, thanks to his own love."[244]

The question, "Does Love/eros pertain only to heterosexual human beings?" presupposes limits to the creative power of the First Person of the Trinity. Love/eros is present in the human condition[245] unconditionally.[246] As of the instant of the Virgin Mary's fiat, human manifestations of "God as Love" are bound only by the Law of the New Covenant, established by Jesus Himself.

> "In the beginning was the Word: the Word was with God and the Word was God. He was with God in the beginning."[247]

That Divine presence defines us as sons of God and of the Virgin Mary; brothers and sisters of her son Jesus. The presence of Divine Love in all human beings restores mankind to its preternatural condition[248]. The Virgin Mary's revolution is complete: we were slaves to sin and now we have been restored as God's heirs, the Mystical Body of Christ.

Four dimensions of Love that emerge in everyone's life are life, pleasure, suffering, and death. The Virgin Mary's revolution endows each of them with a deeper, divinized significance for us. A brief look at each of them serves to recapitulate Part I of this study and to bring it to an end.

## The Annunciation of Life.

Evolution developed all the biological reproductive systems on Earth. At the animal level, we reproduce our species by complementary sexuality. At the specifically human level, the reproduction of Love among us[249] — in *any and all* of its manifestations — eventually takes precedence over its mere biological functions. However, Evolution does not explain to anyone's complete satisfaction the emergence of intelligence and free will in human beings.

At one moment of time, the evolutionary process was altered by the Spirit that created it. In C. S. Lewis' words, "an interference with Nature by a supernatural power"[250] took place. Lewis calls such interference a "miracle," an event caused "by the activity of God," whose "results follow according to Natural law."[251] A Supernatural Power/Energy interfered in time and space and human beings evolved from Nature:

> "Certainly one can debate the details of this formulation;[252] yet the decisive point seems to me to be grasped quite accurately.... If one chooses the second alternative, *it is clear that the spirit is not a random product of material developments, but rather that matter signifies a moment in the history of spirit.* This, however, is just another way of saying that spirit is created and not the mere product of development, even though it comes to light by way of development."[253]

Recently, Fr. Dwight Longenecker explained how the tragic death of his grandfather had become a family myth and that valuable lessons have been learned from it. He compares his family's mythological experience to the stories told by Jesus' apostles and friends;[254] "The comparison is illuminating because of the passage of time." An even longer passage of time clarifies more than obscures the Virgin

Mary's revolutionary myth. In Fr. Longenecker's words:

> "The story of the conception of Jesus Christ is admittedly a supernatural story– an angel appears to a girl and she becomes pregnant by an act of God, but this is nothing like the pagan myths. It is much more like the story of my grandfather's death–an ordinary situation is transformed by a supernatural occurrence. This world is interrupted by the other world, and so transformed."[255]

At the Annunciation, the mystery of human life was *transformed* by an act of God. Sexual activities among humans— kisses, caresses, intercourse, "ordinary situations"—became supernatural occurrences, manifestations of God Himself: "No longer is it a question, then, of a 'commandment' imposed from without and calling for the impossible, but rather of a freely-bestowed experience of love from within, a love which by its very nature must then be shared with others. Love grows through love. *Love is "divine" because it comes from God and unites us to God;* through this unifying process it makes us a "we" which transcends our divisions and makes us one, until in the end God is "all in all"(*1 Cor.* 15:28)."[256]

It may sound tautological, but being is what anything is. A being is that which something always is, from its beginning to the end of its existence. A being sustains its own becoming; that is to say, its own life process; it is the permanent substance that changes in time and space. As was explained earlier, what we are in the eternal present begins and sustains our becoming process in time and space. From what we were (presently nothing any longer), we proceed to what we shall be (also presently nothing yet). In other words, being energizes becoming.

In the case of humans, our being is endowed with immaterial instruments such as intelligence and free will that enable us to recognize the Energy of all Creation. That universal, eternal Energy proceeds from the Creator. The Virgin Mary's fiat revealed its name; "The virgin will conceive and give birth to a son and they will call him Emmanuel, a name which means 'God-is-with-us.'"[257] Emmanuel—Jesus identified God with Love in no uncertain terms. The lesson taught us by the rabbi from Nazareth confirmed his mother's message at the Annunciation: each human life results from the intervention of Divine Love

It is the Spirit of Love that creates the souls of allhumans.[258] *Love creates our souls equally free, rational, and loving.* The human soul literally *animates* the matter inherited genetically from our biological parents: in Chesterton's words, "… a man is not a man without his body, just as he is not a man without his soul."[259]

Thanks to the spiritual instruments at our disposal, we learn the natural law as it is written in our hearts. Once we live according to our new identity, universally revealed after the Virgin Mary's consent to Love, all our actions will be those of sons and daughters of God. Guided by Jesus' commandment to love, our sexual life should, as Merton writes:

> "by its very nature be joyous, unconstrained, alive, leisurely, inventive, and full of a special delight which the lovers have learned by experience to create for one another. There is no more beautiful gift of God than the little secret world of creative love and expression in which two persons who have totally surrendered to each other manifest and celebrate their mutual gift. *It is precisely in this spirit of celebration, gratitude, and joy that true purity is found.* The pure heart is not one that is terrified of *eros* but one that, with the confidence and abandon of a child of God, accepts this gift as a sacred trust, for sex, too, is one of the talents Christ has left us to trade with until He returns."[260]

Merton's words evoke *The Song of Songs*, Kierke-gaard's *Purity of Heart Is to Will One Thing*, and Pope Benedict XVI's *Deus Caritas Est*, to mention only the most obvious references in the present pages. We are images of God. Our lives should manifest "God-is-with-us;" we are one in Jesus. Within the sacrament of marriage, the "special delight" Merton discovers in human sexual activities symbolizes the ecstasy reached in simultaneous sexual orgasm, in which lover and beloved become One in Love.

At the instant Mary conceived, "life" no longer referred to the product of biological evolution alone, which is strictly a time/space phenomenon.[261] The eternal has interfered in the temporal; the miracle of God's incarnation has — quite literally — taken place in "the fullness of time." From that moment forward, "life" took on the new meaning revealed by Jesus:

> "I am the way and the truth and the life;"
>
> "In him was life, and that life was the light of men;
>
> "Jesus said to her, 'I am the resurrection and the life. He who believes in me will live, even though he dies;'"
>
> "...his Son Jesus Christ. He is the true God and eternal life."[262]

In the New Covenant, "life" is Jesus Himself, the sacrament of the Eucharist. Also in the New Covenant, the Incarnation of God is "the primary end of the family." The Virgin Mary's revolution restored human life to its original supernatural dimension.

Jesus Himself gives true and valid meaning to the term "life" every time we find it in the *Catechism of the Catholic Church*,[263] specifically in Article 6 , Part Three, chapter III, "The Love of Husband and Wife." Quoting Pope John Paul II, Numeral 2361 confirms the veracity of what we are saying in these words:

> "Sexuality […] is not something simply biological, but concerns the innermost being of the human person as such. It is realized in a truly human way *only* if it is an integral part of the love by which a man and a woman commit themselves totally to one another until death."[264]

Many other references in the *Catechism* reiterate Jesus' message of Love as the ultimate reason for our life and its sexual manifestations. The following examples provide a clearer insight into the meaning of their content when the "procreation of life" is understood as the procreation of Jesus, of "God-is-with-us," as it was announced to the Virgin Mary:

"**2332** Sexuality affects all aspects of the human person in the unity of his body and soul. It specially concerns affectivity, the capacity to love and to procreate, and in a more general way the aptitude for forming bonds of communion with others."

"**2337** […] Sexuality, in which man's belonging to the bodily and biological world is expressed, becomes personal and truly human when it is integrated into the relationship of one person to another, in the complete and lifelong mutual gift of a man and a woman."

"**2361** Sexuality, by means of which man and woman give themselves to one another through the acts which are proper and exclusive to spouses, is not something simply biological, but concerns the innermost being of the human person as such. It is realized in a truly human way only if it is an integral part of the love by which a man and woman commit themselves totally to one another until death" (*Familiaris Consortio*).

"**2367** Called to give <u>life,</u> spouses share in <u>the creative power and fatherhood of God.</u> 'Married couples should regard it as their proper mission <u>to transmit human life</u> and to educate their children; they should realize that they are thereby <u>*cooperating with* the love of *God the Creator,*</u> and are, in a certain sense, its interpreters. They will fulfill this duty with a sense of human and Christian responsibility;'"[265]

The underscored phrases deserve special attention for their proper interpretation according to Jesus' New Covenant:

"I give you a new commandment: love one another; just as I have loved you, you also must love one another. By this love you have for one another, everyone will know that you are my disciples."[266]

Thus, Numeral 2332 describes sexuality in relation to "the capacity to love and to procreate" and "forming bonds of communion with others." The human person described here is the unity of "body and soul," it has no gender: in Christ, "there is neither male nor female."[267] The capacity to love, to procreate, and to form bonds of communion with others define *spiritual* activities and are not of the flesh alone.

Numeral 2337 reaffirms that after the "only be-gotten Son of God [...] by the Holy Spirit was incar-nate of the Virgin Mary and became man," sexuality becomes *truly human* when integrated to an *interper-sonal* relationship. Since we are created in God's im-age, that relationship reflects the "life" of the Trini-ty. The last part of the numeral, i.e. "the complete and lifelong mutual gift of a man and a woman," introduces gender into the sexual relationship. This contradicts the concept of "human person" as the unity of body and soul and as the image of our (genderless) Creator.

In Numeral 2361 the mutuality of complimentary sexuality is emphasized once again. The *sacrament* of marriage is explained, in which a man and a woman give themselves to one another. Even in this sacra-mental context, the *Catechism* reiterates the *spiritual* dimension of human sexuality: "it is realized in a truly human way *only* if it is an integral part of the love...."

Of the numerals mentioned here, #2367 lends it-self to the materialistic interpretation of human sex-uality (the procreation of children). Many thinkers may identify the reason for this common misinter-pretation as the Tradition of the Church, her Magis-terium, or the Old Covenant. The life to which

*The Catechism* refers is "not something simply biological," as Pope John Paul II wrote in *Familiaris Consortio.* The "creative power and fatherhood of God" are not revealed in the evolutionary process He created billions of years ago, but in the eternal present, in which His miracles occur. "Cooperating with the love of God the Creator" is not a material, physical enterprize but simply another dimension of the single reality that is Love. Married couples, single persons, consecrated virgins, celibate persons, in sum, *all of us*, should regard as our "proper mission to transmit human life," which we know by faith to be the life of Christ.[268]

### Pleasure, a Dimension of Love

"As a youth I had been woefully at fault,particularly in early adolescence.[269] I had prayed to you for chastity and said 'Give me chastity and continence, but not yet.' For I was afraid that you would answer my prayer at once and cure me too soon of the disease of lust, which I wanted satisfied, not quelled." (St. Augustine)[270]

St. Augustine's prayer asking God to heal his "disease of lust" could be that of a present day Christian Scientist. Fortunately, having overcome

**St. Augustine of Hippo.**

his Manichean past, this Doctor of the Church was able to explain in his *Confessions* that lust is a *spiritual* affliction. In turn, that affliction has physical consequences other than the ephemeral pleasures derived from satisfying never-ending sensual appetites.

> "Many years of my life had passed — twelve, unless I am wrong — since I had read Cicero's *Hortensius* at the age of nineteen and it had inspired me to study philosophy. But I still postponed my renunciation of this world's joys..."[271]
>
> -- St. Augustine

Hannah Arendt's doctoral dissertation, *Der Liebesbegriff bei Augustin*[272] is among the best philosophical studies of Divine Love as described by the author of *Confessions*. In Part I, "Love as Craving, the Anticipated Future," she describes how *caritas* and *cupiditas* derive from craving desire (*appetitus*), a manifestation of love. "*Cupiditas*," Arendt held, makes us "denizens of this world," while "*caritas*" grants us citizenship in the world-to-come. Saint Augustine himself, "could see no certain goal towards which I might steer my course." The saint proceeded to hide behind his contrived uncertainty,[273] keeping God away from his "innermost being."

But happiness occurs when "the gap between lover and beloved has been closed."[274] Once the dichotomy Love-lust is resolved and we choose *caritas* (appetite for eternal Love) over *cupiditas* (appetite for things of this world), only then will our hearts find peace and rest in Love.[275]

Finally, *mutatis mutandis*, St. Thomas Aquinas deals with our hearts' operations also in *De Motu Cordis*:[276]

> "In the same way, it is natural to man that his appetite to seek his ultimate goal which is his happiness and to shun misery.[...] Therefore since the motion of

> all other members are caused by the
> motion of the heart...other motions can be
> voluntary, but *the first motion, which is that
> of the heart, is natural.*"[277]

As mentioned earlier, it is the total giving of ourselves that creates our sexual pleasure. When through our sexual actions we give ourselves to Love, Love satisfies us *in eternity*, not just "for the time being." In Love, sexual acts unify subject/lover, object/beloved, and verb/Love. In the Spirit of Love, our sexual activities are, quite literally, acts of Divine Love; they provide sanctifying grace. In what must be the most egregious understatement of the *Catechism*, numeral 2362 affirms that "Sexuality is a source of joy and pleasure:

> "The Creator himself ... established
> that in the [generative] function,
> spouses should experience pleasure
> and enjoyment of body and spirit.
> Therefore, the spouses do nothing
> evil in seeking this pleasure and en-
> joyment. They accept what the Cre-
> ator has intended for them."[278]

These words foreshadow those of Father Fuchs, spiritual director of Pius XII:

> "... what God wants is not 'sexual activa-
> tion according to sexuality as such' but

'sexual activation, indeed according to its particular nature, yet above all sexual activation of the whole human being,' according to its nature as a *person*."[279]

Of course, it could argued that Fr. Fuchs had no way of knowing "what God wants," anymore than he knew that "The Pope was thinking…" on a related issue.[280] However, as his spiritual director, Fr. Fuchs did know the Pope's mind, and as a professor of moral theology his knowledge of natural law was unsurpassed.

The pleasures inherent in human sexual activities are divine indications that happiness consists in the fulfillment of that "most perfect of animals which is man."[281]

### Suffering and Death

"Without death, life becomes meaningless."[282]

None of the accounts of the Annunciation, in the Bible or in the Qur'an, describe the suffering of the Virgin Mary upon accepting her Divine Lover's proposal. Other than amazement and wander, the young virgin experienced fear, perhaps bordering on panic; "She was *deeply disturbed* by these words and asked herself what this greeting could mean…"

Uncontrolled fear is the prologue of terror; however, Mary was spared that experience. As it always does, Love set her heart at peace."The angel said to her, 'Mary, do not be afraid; you have won God's favor'." Winning "God's favor" meant being impregnated by the Creative Spirit of her Divine Lover.

The good news elated the Virgin Mary, as was manifested in the *Magnificat*:[283] "My soul magnifies the Lord/And my spirit rejoices in  God my Savior; Because he has regarded the lowliness of his handmaid; For behold, henceforth all generations shall call me blessed; Because he who is mighty has done great things for me, and holy is his name; And his mercy is from generation to generation on those who fear Him."

Love's elation may have subdued her fears, but—again, as always—not her suffering. Mary learned that the New Covenant, the law of Love proclaimed by Her Son, entailed suffering in this world. The *Catechism* summarizes this truth:

"The world we live in often seems very far from the one promised us by faith. Our experiences of evil and suffering, injustice, and death, seem to contradict the Good News; they shake our faith and become a temptation against it.

It is then we must turn to the *witnesses of faith*: to Abraham... to *the Virgin Mary, who, in 'her pilgrimage of faith,' walked*

> *the 'night of faith'* in sharing her son's suf-
> fering and death...."[284]

Even with a "shaken" faith, we, Mary and the Church, understand that "Our experiences of evil and suffering" have been redefined after she rejected the Mosaic Laws. The Virgin Mary's revolution restored our original condition of sons of her Divine Lover. One in Christ, we are now His Body, the Church.

Beginning at the Annunciation, Love revealed the redemptive nature of human suffering; e.g., fear of the Lord now becomes respect for our Father. The Virgin Mary's Son transforms suffering into a manifestation of Love and death is no longer the end of life but rather the beginning of Life.[285] Only by loving unto death do we transcend this life.[286]

## The Eucharist

Through His suffering and death Jesus restores us to Paradise;[287] the old laws are no longer relevant. Now, it is *the New Covenant that binds humanity to God,* a covenant sealed not with the blood of Abraham's circumcision[288] but with Christ's crucifixion. Out of love of his Father, He shed it completely for us, as we are reminded in the liturgy of the Holy Mass: "Take and drink ye all of this, for this is the chalice of my blood, of the new and eternal testament...."[289]

In summary, we are well aware of the perennial complaint of peoples who have suffered greatly "for "no apparent reasons." Harold S. Kushner's book *When Bad Things Happen to Good People*, published over 3 decades ago, was an attempt to find a reasonable explanation to the mystery of the human condition.[290] The history of humanity and the diverse mythological accounts of our beginnings always include Suffering and Death.[291]

From one culture to another the only difference is how they are interpreted. Thus, for example, in the Judeo-Christian-Islamic cultures, suffering accounts in part for purification of the individual, while death, marks the final stage of that individual's return journey to the Father.[292] A careful reading of the story of the return of the prodigal son is a near-perfect illustration of the meaning of suffering and death under the new law of the Father's Love.

The only way to transcend suffering and death is by "embracing" them[293] and loving one another as the Father loves us, *always and unconditionally.*

**Return of the Prodigal Son**

"It was the best of times, it was the worst of times, it was the age of wisdom, it was the age of foolishness, it was the epoch of belief, it was the epoch of incredulity, it was the season of Light, it was the season of Darkness, it was the spring of hope, it was the winter of despair, we had everything before us, we had nothing before us, we were all going direct to Heaven, we were all going direct the other way—in short, *the period was so far like the present period,* that some of its noisiest authorities insisted on its being received, for good or for evil, in the superlative degree of comparison only."[294]

## EPILOGUE

Regarding the Virgin Mary's revolution, our choices are clear:

1. Believe or not believe Mary's story as she told it;
2. Accept the consequences of your faith as Mary did, or adhere to the Old Covenant;
3. Accept the guidance of Love or adopt idolatry as a religion.

Are the title and the subtitle of this book justified? Once the term "revolution" is defined accurately, the answer suggests itself. Hannah Arendt's definition of revolution (see Appendix 1) helps us understand how it was that at the Annunciation the Virgin Mary started a completely new and different stage for the evolution of humanity.

In brief, a revolution is a movement in which the mover is also the object moved as well as the energy of the motion. In other words, a revolution changes the subject executing it, thereby completely restoring itself to its original rightful state.

Thus, in the Virgin Mary's revolution, she is the subject whose actions release us from the Old Covenant and bring about the New. The love of God completely restores the world.[295] *Eros*/Love rules.

> "It is neither the spirit alone nor the body alone that loves: it is man, the person, a unified creature composed of body and soul, who loves. Only when both dimensions are truly united, does man attain his full stature. Only thus is love —*eros*—able to mature and attain its authentic grandeur."[296]

Gonzalo T. Palacios was born in Maracay, Venezuela (1938). He studied architecture (Catholic University of America in Washington DC and Universidad Central in Caracas). He received his MA in Philosophy from the Gregorian University (Rome) and his Ph.D. from the Catholic University of America. During his 25 years as an accredited diplomat to the White House, Dr. Palacios founded the Association of Iberoamerican Cultural Attaches. Presently he teaches philosophy at Prince George's Community College and presides over the Erasmus Group, dedicated to the discussion of issues such as Darwinian evolution and free will.

## APPENDIX I: On Revolution

Although she was writing primarily on political philosophy, the following excerpts from Hannah Arendt's essay *On Revolution*[297] may clarify the significance of the term "revolution," as in *The Virgin Mary's Revolution* and as used by Pope Benedict XVI recently. Comments in italics.

1. "The word 'revolutionary' can be applied only to revolutions whose aim is freedom;" Arendt quotes Antoine Nicolas de Condorcet's «Sur le sens du mot Révolutionnaire» (1793), in *Œuvres*, Paris, 1847-9), vol. XII; Arendt, page 29. *As was later revealed by her Son, the Virgin Mary's revolution had one basic objective, to liberate humanity from the shackles of sin, especially the sin of idolatry.*

2. "... only where change occurs in the sense of a new beginning, where violence is used to constitute an altogether different form of government, to bring about the formation of a new body politic, where the liberation from oppression aims at least at the constitution of freedom can we speak of revolution." Arendt, page 35. *The Annunciation ushered a new beginning for the human race, "a new body poli-*

*tic,"the Mystical Body of Christ. Jesus declared Love to be "the different form of government."* "The vocation to sanctity and communion with God is part of His eternal plan, a plan which stretches over history and which *includes all the men and women of the world*, because the call is universal. God excludes no one, His plan is exclusively a plan of love." Benedict XVI, Vatican City, 20 June 2012 (VIS).

3. "The word 'revolution' was originally an astronomical term [Copernicus' *De revolutionum orbium coelestium*] ...it clearly indicates a recurring, cyclical movement... an eternal, irresistible , ever-recurring motion to the haphazard movements, the ups and downs of human destiny... The fact [is] that the word 'revolution' meant originally restoration... The revolutions of the seventeenth and eighteenth centuries, which to us appear to show all evidence of a new spirit...were intended to be restorations." Arendt, pages 42-43. *The revolution of the Virgin Mary restored humanity to its Divine Creator. "I and the Father are one," Jesus declares (John; 10, 30) and later, He reveals that He has restored humanity and Creation at large to our Father.*

4. "In Tocqueville's words, 'one might have believed the aim of the coming revolution was not the overthrow of the old regime but its restoration.'" *L'Ancien Régime,* Paris, 1953, vol. II, p. 72; Arendt, 287, note 28. *Christ restored the original intent of the Mosaic Law (Love God) instituting the New Covenant, the Law of Love.*

# ENDNOTES

[1] http://www.readability.com/articles/n9vv2acs.

[2] For example, FOX TV commentator Rush Limbaugh called Sandra Fluke 'a slut' — and had to apologize for his insult. What would Mr. Limbaugh call the Virgin Mary today? abcnews.go.com Politics OTUS News Mar 3, 2012.

[3] According to St. Thomas Aquinas (II-II, Q. liii, a. 1).

[4] *On the Soul,* Book II, chapters 3 & 4.

[5] *On the Soul,* Book II, chapter 3, 414 B 20.

[6] Michael Novak, *The Experience of Nothingness,* 1971, Chapter II, #3 "The Drive to Raise Questions".

[7] Paul Tillich, *The Courage to Be,* 1952; pages 48 and 121.

[8] *Summa Theologica* III, 68, Art. 11.

[9] Rand, *The Virtue of selfishness,* chapter 1.

[10] "Once profit becomes the exclusive goal, if it is produced by improper means and without the common good as its ultimate end, it risks destroying wealth and creating poverty." Benedict XVI, *Deus Caritas Est,* Chapter 2, 21.

[11] http://en.wikipedia.org/wiki/History_of_brassieres#cite_ref-58.

[12] www.facebook.com/note.php?note_id=334955273273.

[13] *U.S. News & World Report,* 9/15-22/2008, page 52.

[14] *Totem and Taboo: Resemblances between the Psychic Lives of Savages and Neurotics by* Dr. Sigmund Freud, LL.D. Authorized English Translation with Introduction by A. A. BRILL, Ph.D., M.D. The Savages Dread of Incest, in <http//archive.org/details/totemtabooresemb00freu>.

[15] (Agamemnom, *strophe iii).*

[16] *Twilight of the Idols*,1888.

[17] The Pope Warns Against the Danger of False Religiosity: Vatican City, 3 September 2012 (VIS).

[18] The Peripatetic axiom is: "Nothing is in the intellect that was not first in the senses" (Latin: "Nihil est in intellectu quod non prius in sensu").

[19] Dorothy L. Sayers in *The Mind of the Maker.*

[20] The Triune God.

[21] See www.youtube.com/watch?feature=endscreen&NR =1&v=6De9SFc2jhU.

[22] *On the soul*, II, 3, 415 A 28.

[23] See Appendix "On Revolution."

[24] John Urwin, "One of the Many Quirks of Quantum: Perpetual Motion and Never-ending Currents," in *Yale Scientific*, April 2012: my italics.

[25] *The Life of the Mind*, II, 123.

[26] Aristotle, *Protreptikos*, 1072a21.

[27] *St. Basil of Caesarea,* Letter 233.

[28] *Sermon II on the New Testament*,17.

[29] http://main.zerotothree.org/site/PageServer?pagename=ter _key_brainFAQ.

[30] *Ethics*, 1168 A 19

[31] *Estudios sobre el Amor,* pag. 68.

[32] Stephen C. Meyer, *Signature in the Cell, DNA and the evidence for intelligent design*, Harper One, 2009; page 12.

[33] *On the soul*, II, 3, 415 A 28.

[34] *The God Delusion,* 2006, p.199.

[35] *On St. John's Gospel, Tractatus 36, # 7.*

[36] This is the case in Islam: their truth is to be found solely in the Holy Qu'ram *as written originally*, not to be interpreted or subjected to temporal circumstances.

[37] "Development means that each thing expands to be itself, while alteration means that a thing is changed from one thing into another," *Paganism and Christianity*, 10/12, 2012 By Fr. Dwight Longenecker.

[38] In this text, the term 'myth' is equivalent to 'story,' used to describe a mystery or a mystical event.

[39] Pope John Paul II, *Ut unum sint,* May 1995.

[40] Jacques Derrida, *The Gift of Death*, 45: my italics.

[41] Jacob Needleman, "The Great Unknown is Me, Myself," *Parabola*, Fall 2012.

[42] "Socrates shows that the true lover is the lover of the soul…" Robert R. Wellman, "Socrates and Alcibiades: The Alcibiades the Major."
http://www.blissofpeace.com/socrates/Alcibiades.PDF .

[43] Bruce Barton, *What Can a Man Believe?* Bobbs-Merrill Co., 1927, page 156: "I know that my intelligence (and by *me* I mean mankind) is the highest and most powerful thing in the natural universe."

[44] Barton, page 157, my emphasis.

[45] Where "manifestations themselves are equated to their Eternal Creator; see page 36, above.

[46] Stephen Hawkins, *The Grand Design,* 2010.

[47] http://www.ncregister.com/site/print_article/33888/ .

[48] in *The Everlasting Man*, my italics.

[49] Other consequences appear in Part 3.

[50] *A young man in search of Love*, 1978; 137.

[51] Pope Benedict XVI, Sunday, April 29, 2012.

[52] "Yet *eros* and *agape*—ascending love and descending love—can never be completely separated;" Benedict XVI, *Deus Caritas Est*, Part 1, # 7. Since the words "erotic love" have lost their original meaning, the term "Love-*eros*" is used to designate the presence of the Creator in the human person. "Today, the term

"love" has become one of the most frequently used and mis-used of words, a word to which we attach quite different meanings;" Benedict XVI, *op. cit* Part I, # 2.

[53] See Chapter 3: My Generation's Sexual Revolution, page 16 above,

[54] See *The McDonaldization of Sex*, by Tim Muldoon, http://www.patheos.com/Catholic/McDonaldization-Sex-Tim-Muldoon-06-19-2012.html

[55] *Song of Songs,* chapter 2

[56] Martin Luther King, Jr., *Letter from a Birmingham Jail.*

[57] "it is a unity which creates love, a unity in which both God and man remain themselves and yet become fully one. As Saint Paul says: "He who is united to the Lord becomes one spirit with him" (*1 Cor* 6:17); Benedict XVI, *Deus Caritas Est.*

[58] "'Shall I conceal from Abraham what I am going to do, see-ing that Abraham will become a great nation with all the na-tions of the earth blessing themselves by him?'" *Genesis*; 18, 16. It is significant that this allusion to the precursor of the Church, i.e., Israel, comes immediately after another "annun-ciation" of a miraculous pregnancy, that of Sara.

[59] *Deuteronomy,* xxii. 24, circa 700 B.C.

[60] http://www.washingtonpost.com/opinions/chen-guangcheng-will-chinese-justice-rescue-my-detained-nephew/2012/06/19/gJQAOk1LoV_story.html

[61] www.americanbar.org/groups/domestic_violence/.../statistics.html

[62] Luke 1, 43 +.

[63] *John* 2:1–11. Read more: http://www.ncregister.com/blog/mark-shea/the-significance-of-the-wedding-at-cana#ixzz265Wg9JiL

[64] *John* 8, 7-11.

[65] *John* 10; 30.

66 *Mutatis mutandis,* "faith removes nothing from the human creature, rather it permits his full and final realization;" Pope Benedict XVI in Loreto, Italy, October 4, 2012 (see end of Part II, page 39).

67 William Wordsworth, *My heart leaps up.*

68 *Hamlet,* I, v.

69 *The Ancient City,* Chapter 8 "Authority in the family," Doubleday Anchor Books, page 88.

70 Howard Markel, *An Anatomy of Addiction, Sigmund Freud, William Halsted, and the miracle drug Cocaine,* Pantheon Books, 2011, page 186. Also, see Freud's *The Interpretation of Dreams,* 2nd ed., Preface.

71 Stephen Hawkins, page 38 above.

72 *De Potentia Dei,* q. 5, a. 1, ad. 2.

73 "*Thomas Aquinas and Big Bang Cosmology*" by William Carroll http://maritain.nd.edu/jmc/ti/carroll.htm.

74 Such denial is absurd if one understands that evolution is another name for the Second Person of the Trinity: "Through him all things came to be, not one thing had its being but through him," *John,* 1; 3.

75 *Sûrah* 71, 13-18.

76 *Symposium,* 190 C-D.

77 Saint Augustine, *Confessions,* Book XI, 1.

78 John Donne, *Devotions Upon Emergent Occasions,* "Meditation XVII".

79 *Mary, the New Eve,* by Rev. Matthew R. Mauriello http://campus.udayton.edu/mary/meditations/neweve.html In other words, Jesus was the *begotten, not made,* Son of God.

80 Fr. Robert Barron, Herman Lecture, 2012, Just Quietly Productions, the John Paul II Institute, Washington DC; minutes 22-23. The Arabic word "*halaqa*" means a gathering for the primary purpose of learning about God: this word has been transcribed phonetically and it could be the word *ahabà*, which

the Greek version of the Old Testament translates with the similar-sounding *agape*, BXVI *Deus Caritas Est*, I, 6.

[81] "The answer may exist somewhere in the midst of the fourth century, when Christianity morphed from a freakish band of outsiders seeking justice for the disenfranchised to the religion of the Empire and Emperors;" in Lisa Miller's "Why is the woman so often the only victim?", *The Washington Post*, 11-17=2012, B2.

[82] "The New Men," in *Mere Christianity*, page 184.

[83] *Hamlet*, V, 2.

[84] *Acts*, 2; 4. "The Spirit gave them gift of speech:" does this gift relate to our First Amendment? See above, pages 42-43.

[85] Werner Jaeger, *Early Christianity and Greek Paideia*, 1961.

[86] *John 2; 6.*

[87] Letter to St. Ignatius of Loyola, Rome, 1543).
http://www.fordham.edu/halsall/mod/1543xavier1.asp

[88] *John*, 19; 27.

[89] *Luke*, 8; 21.

[90] Appendix , "On Revolution."

[91] *John*, 15; 14-15. Also, "Love of God and love of neighbor are thus inseparable, they form a single commandment. But both live from the love of God who has loved us first. No longer is it a question, then, of a "commandment" imposed from with-out and calling for the impossible, but rather of a freely-bestowed experience of love from within, a love which by its very nature must then be shared with others. Love grows through love. Love is "divine" because it comes from God and unites us to God; through this unifying process it makes us a "we" which transcends our divisions and makes us one, until in the end God is "all in all" (*1 Cor* 15:28); Benedict XVI, *Deus Caritas Est*, 1, 18.

[92] St. Augustine, *On Sacred Virginity,* 6.

[93] Emphasis added; Thomas Merton, "Rebirth and the New Man in Christianity," in *Love and Living,* 1981, page 174.

[94] Thomas Merton, *Love and Living,* Bantam Book, 1981, page 104.

[95] *Acts,* 1; 8.

[96] "But from the time Constantine legalized Christianity throughout Rome, the faith from which so many of our cultural assumptions still spring favored and protected men and preserved the invisibility and impotence especially of married women." In Lisa Miller's "Why is the woman so often the only victim?" See note 85.

[97] *The Washington Post,* 06-26-2012.

[98] "Kate's breasts, Pussy Riot, virginity tests and our attitude on women's bodies" by Naomi Wolf, CNN Wed September 19, 2012.

[99] A character in Lampedusa's *Il Gattopardo*.

[100] *"Se vogliamo che tutto rimanga come è, bisogna che tutto cambi."*

[101] See Chapter 17, "True Revolution." Above, page 38.

[102] "Muhammad, the founder of Islam, was his own Constantine. During his lifetime, Islam became a political as well as a religious allegiance, and the Prophet's community in Medina became a state with the Prophet himself as sovereign...." Bernard Lewis, *The Middle East,* Scribner, NY, 1995, page 138.

[103] http://www.discoverthenetworks.org/default.asp .

[104] See Abdelwahab Bouhdiba, *Sexuality in Islam*, translated from the French by Alan Sheridan, London, 1974, Chapter X, "Variations of erotism, misogyny, mysticism, and mujum (lust)"

[105] "...how it has come about that the Church has reached such great temporal power..."; N. Machiavelli, *The Prince*, Chapter XI, "Of Ecclesiastical Principalities." Also, "They [the Jesuits] are simply the Romish army for the earthly sovereignty of the world in the future, with the Pontiff of Rome for Emperor [...] do you really think the Roman Catholic movement of the last centuries is actually nothing but the lust for power, for filthy earthly gain?" in F. Dostoevsky, *The Brothers Karamazov*, Book V, chapter 5, "The Grand Inquisitor."

[106] Merton, page 181.

[107] *Romans*, 13, 1, 2.

[108] "Then Peter stood up with the Eleven and addressed them in a loud voice: […] 'In the days to come – it is the Lord who speaks - I will pour out my spirit *to all mankind;'" Acts*, 2; 14-17.

[109] *Genesis*, 17; 1-12.

[110] *Luke*, 22: 20.

[111] "One of the soldiers pierced his side with a lance; and immediately there came out blood and water" *John*, 19; 34-35: is this a reference to the miracle at Cana?

[112] *John,* 19; 30.

[113] *John*, 20; 22.

[114] *Col.* 2; 14-15.

[115] *John* 13; 34-35.

[116] *Revelation;* 20: 2-6

[117] The eternal Word: "The Fathers of the Council *to All Men*: We take great pleasure in sending *to all men* and nations a message concerning that well-being (*salutis*), love, and peace which were *brought into the world* by Jesus Christ, the Son of the living God, and entrusted to the Church;" *Message to Humanity*, opening of the Second Vatican Council, October 20, 1962.

[118] St. Paul, *Romans*, 7; 4-6.

[119] *The Song of Songs*, 7; 10 – 14.

[120] Joseph Campbell, *Mythic Worlds, Modern Words, on the art of James Joyce,* HarperCollins, 1993, page 23.

[121] *Deus Caritas Est*, Part I, # 5.

[122] This is the definition of a sacrament.

[123] "His mother stored up all these things in her heart. And Jesus increased in wisdom, in stature, and in favor with God and men;" *Luke*, 2; 52.

[124] Ineffabilis Deus of 8 December, 1854, Pius IX pronounced and defined that the Blessed Virgin Mary "in the first instance of her conception, by a singular privilege and grace granted by God, in view of the merits of Jesus Christ, the Savior of the human race, was preserved exempt from all stain of original sin," *The Catholic Encyclopedia.*

[125] *Mt* 22: 37-40.

[126] Benedict XVI: God's Revolutionary by Samuel Gregg, in *Crisis Magazine,* April 16, 2012.

[127] See <*smarthistory.khanacademy.org/michelangelo-pieta.html*>

[128] *Deus Caritas Est,* Part I, # 5.

[129] *Luke* 1; 34-35.

[130] *Mutatis mutandis,* "The term 'conception does not mean the active or generative conception by her parents. Her body was formed in the womb of the mother, and the father had the usual share in its formation. The question does not concern the immaculateness of the generative activity of her parents. Neither does it concern the passive conception absolutely and simply which, according to the order of nature, precedes the infusion of the rational soul. The person is truly conceived when the soul is created and infused into the body." *The Catholic Encyclopedia;* "Immaculate Conception".

[131] *Revelation,* 12; 1-3.

[132] *Revelation,* 12; 5.

[133] Premiered in Paris, Théâtre du Vieux-Colombier, May, 1944.

[134] *Matthew,* 22; 37-40.

[135] *Revelation,* 12; 17.

[136] Benedict XVI talks of True Revolution to Youth, http:/zenith.org/article-13762?1. Also, Note 118, page 71.

[137] Plato, *Symposium,* 178 a -179 b.

[138] *Theogony* 116 seq.

[139] Latin for "the ascent of the mind to wisdom" and Italian for "loving use of wisdom" respectively; in The Treatment Of Poetry In The Symposium Of Plato, iv, page 54, by Paul Epstein pde7229@okstate.edu.

[140] *Symposium*, 178 c-d.

[141] Wetherbee, Winthrop, "Dante Alighieri", *The Stanford Encyclopedia of Philosophy (Winter 2011 Edition)*, Edward N. Zalta (ed.), URL = http://plato.stanford.edu/archives/win2011/entries/dante/>.

[142] *The Decameron,* Epilog, # 5.

[143] *Ibid.,* # 1.

[144] *1 John*, 4; 7-20.

[145] *A l'alta fantasia qui mancò possa;/ ma già volgeva il mio disio e 'l velle,/ sì come rota ch' igualmente è mossa,/ l'Amor che move il sole e l'altre stelle*: "Paradiso" Canto 33, cxlii-cxlv (my translation).

[146] *La gloria di Colui che tutto move/ per l'universo penetra, e risplende/ in una parte più e meno altrove*: "Paradiso," Canto 1, i-iv (my translation).

[147] *Revelation*; 22, 13.

[148] *Love in the Western World,* Pantheon Books, 1956.

[149] Benedict XVI, *Deus Caritas Est;* # 3; "eros" and "agape" – difference and unity.

[150] De Rougemont, page 62.

[151] Ortega y Gasset, *Estudios sobre el Amor*, 15th ed., Revista de Occidente, Madrid,, 1964; page 75.

[152] Plato, *Ion*, 533 C -535 A.

[153] *Luke* 22:19-20, *Matthew* 26:26-28, *Mark* 14:22-24, *John* 6:58-59, *1 Corinthians* 11:23-25.

[154] *Luke* 23: 46.

[155] Benedict XVI, Loreto, 10-04-2012.

[156] "…it is neither the spirit alone nor the body alone that loves: it is man, the person, a unified creature composed of body and soul, who loves. Only when both dimensions are truly united, does man attain his full stature. Only thus is love —eros—able to mature and attain its authentic grandeur." Benedict XVI, *op. cit.* Part 1, # 5.

[157] *Deuteronomy* 6: 4-5; *Leviticus* 19:18. "Since God has first loved us ( *1 Jn* 4: 10), love is now no longer a mere "command"; it is the response to the gift of love with which God draws near us," Benedict XVI in *Deus Caritas Est*, Introduction.

[158] *Deuteronomy* 5:6–18; *Exodus* 19:9; 20:2–14.

[159] Galatians, 4: 4-7. Literally, the "fullness of time;" the messianic age, when "God has sent the Spirit of His Son into our hearts: the Spirit that cries , 'Abba, Father', and it is this that makes you a son, you are not a slave any more…"

[160] The use of past and present tenses in the same sentence is deliberate.

[161] The end of time and space *is* the Present.

[162] Origen called her "worthy of God;" Maximus of Turin, Mary is "a dwelling fit for Christ;" for St. Augustine she was totally without sin. See Appendix 2. Also,God the Holy Ghost knew the immaculate virgin intimately;" Benedict XVI, May 27, 2012.

[163] See Note 91, page 63.

[164] Benedict XVI, Vatican City, 24 November 2012 (VIS).

[165] Louis Roberts, *The Achievement of Karl Rahner*, Herder and Herder, 1967, page 242,

[166] *Catechism of the Catholic Church*, Editrice Vaticana, 1994, page 5.

[167] *Catechism*, # 1325.

[168] *Catechism*, # 1328.

[169] Saint Augustine, *De Civit. Dei*, Book XVI: "Some people, in order to discover God, read books. But there is a great book: the very appearance of created things. Look above you! Look below you! Note it. Read it. God, whom you want to discover, never wrote that book with ink. Instead He set before your eyes the things that He had made. Can you ask for a louder voice than that? Why, heaven and earth shout to you: "God made me!"

[170] In http://www.bookofnature.org/library/ngb.htm.

[171] Margaret A. Farley, *Just Love: A Framework for Christian Sexual Ethics*, Continuum, N.Y., 2007, page 37.

[172] *Ibid.*

[173] "Freud & Humanist Judaism", Dr Ian Ridgway PhD in http://www.myauz.com/ianr/articles/lect4freud%20&hHu manistjudaism07.pdf

[174] "How did Jesus view the Old Testament?" Josh McDowell, from *Reasons Skeptics Should Consider Christianity* Tyndale House, 1981.

[175] *Luke*, 22; 20

[176] *Matthew* 19: 21.

[177] "Sex outside of marriage (...) has generally been forbidden or at least discouraged (...) Masturbation, incest, adultery, male homosexuality, have all been considered serious transgressions. Lesbian relations were not regulated by biblical law...", Farley, p. 36.

[178] "Purity of heart is to will one thing. .For commitment to the Good is a whole-souled decision ...since God is spirit and truth, a man can only draw near to Him by sincerity, by willing to be holy, as He is holy; *by purity of heart.*" Soren Kierkergaard, *Purity of Heart is to will one thing*, Fontana books, 1961, page 154.

[179] "On the day of the Annunciation, Mary was "deep in thought and yet ready to listen to God. There was no obstacle within her, no barrier, nothing that would separate her from God. This is the meaning of her being without original sin. Her relationship with God is free from even the slightest rift; there is no separation, no shadow of selfishness, but rather perfect harmony. Her little human heart was perfectly 'centred' in the great heart of God. [...] the voice of God is not recognised amid noise and turmoil; his plan for our life as individuals and as a society are not visible on the surface; we need to descend to a deeper level where the forces at work are not economic or political but moral and spiritual. It is at this deeper level that Mary invites us to enter into harmony with God's action," Benedict XVI, *The Power of Grace is Stronger than Evil*, Vatican City, 8 December 2012 (VIS).

[180] In all religions, Benedict XVI tells us, "*Eros* was thus celebrated as divine power, as fellowship with the Divine," *D.c.e.*, 1, #4.

[181] "...the heart of the Christian faith [is] the Christian image of God and the resulting image of mankind and its destiny;" Benedict XVI, *D.c.e.*, Part I, preamble.

[182] Leo J. Latz, *The Rhythm of Sterility and Fertility in Women*, 6th edition, Latz Foundation, 1942, page122.

[183] "True, *eros* tends to rise "in ecstasy" towards the Divine, to lead us beyond ourselves;" Benedict XVI, *D.c.e.*, 1, #5. At the Annunciation, YHW's command in *Genesis* 9; 7 to "be fruitful and multiply" refers to the procreation and multiplication of Love.

[184] *John* 13; 34-35.

[185] Indra Sinha, "Kama Sutra" in Wikipedia.

[186] Vatsyayana, *Kama Sutra, the Hindu Ritual of Love*, Castle Books, N.Y., 1963, page 10.

[187] See Note 126, page 73 above and Part One, chapter 3, page 16 above.

[188] Abdelwahab Bouhdiba, *La Sexiualidad en el Islam,* Monteavila, Caracas, 1980, page 26.

[189] Brian Lewis, *The Middle East, A Brief History of the Last 2,000 Years,* Scribner, N.Y., 1995, page 53.

[190] Vali Nasr, *The Shia Revival, How Conflict within Islam Will Shape the Future*, W. W. Norton, N.Y., 2006, page 29.

[191] Sûrah 4, # 34, *The Qur'an.*

[192] Sûrah 66, # 1.

[193] *Deus caritas est*, "Love of God and love of neighbor," Part I, 16.

[194] *1 Timothy* 1; 11. The Catechism quotes the previous verse, 1; 10, in which St. Paul explains the reach of the Mosaic Law rather than the New Covenant or the Law of Love.

[195] See "Sin contra naturam," Robert L.A. Clark, *Encyclopedia of Sex and Gender, V. 4. Detroit: Macmillan Reference USA, 2007. http://www.omnilogos.com/2011/10/04/sin-contra-naturam/*.

[196] Howard Kainz, "Homosexuality, Civil Rights, and Natural Law," in http://www.thecatholicthing.org/columns/2011/homosexuality-civil-rights-and-natural-law.html.

[197] Kainz, *loc. cit.*

[198] Kainz, *loc. cit.*

[199] Fuchs, *op. cit.,* page 143, note 27.

[200] Kainz, *ibidem.*

[201] Fuchs, *op. cit.,* page 175; emphasis added.

[202] *Deus Caritas Est,* I, # 7.

[203] Like most of what has been stated in this essay, this thought on chastity is Catholic tradition. In Novenberoff 2007 Fr. Richard John Neuhaus quoted the American Bishops to the effect that "All people, whether married or single, are called to chaste living. Chaste living overcomes disordered human desires such as lust and results in the expression **of one's sexual desires in harmony with God's will...**" in "Ministry to Persons with a Homosexual Inclination: Guidelines for Pastoral Care."

[204] *Galatians*, 5; 22-24. Saint Paul uses the Greek εγκρατεια (egkrateia) for "self-control", a word used by Xenophon and popularized by Plato's Socrates in *The Apology* and *Republic*. Self-control was the foundation of all virtues and an essential condition to being a good ruler: See Werner Jaeger, *Paideia, the Ideals of Greek Culture,* Book II, chapter 2, "Socrates educator," *per corpus.*

[205] *John* 19:25-27.

[206] *John* 19:25-27.

[207] *Matthew* 12:46-50. "The words addressed by the crucified Lord to his disciple—to John and through him to all disciples of Jesus: "Behold, your mother!" (*Jn* 19:27)—are fulfilled anew in every generation. Mary has truly become the Mother of all believers." Benedict XVI, *Deus Caritas Est*, Conclusion, # 42.

[208] "A new command I give you: Love one another. As I have loved you, so you must love one another. By this everyone will know that you are my disciples..." *John*, 13; 34-35.

[209] "*Yo soy yo y mi circunstancia, y si no la salvo a ella no me salvo yo*"; José Ortega y Gasset, *Meditaciones del Quijote*, Revista de Occidente,  1963, página 18.

[210] *The Phenomenon of Man, with an introduction by Sir Julian Huxley*, Harper Colophon Books, N.Y., 1965, page 264.

[211] *Deus Caritas est*, Part I, # 4.

[212] *Matthew*  5; 48.

[213] "Since purity must be understood as the correct way of treating the sexual sphere according to one's personal state (and not necessarily absolute abstention from sexual life), then undoubtedly this purity is included in the Pauline concept of self-control or enkrateia." *Life in the Spirit Based on True Freedom* By Pope John Paul II, http://www.catholicnewsagency.com/document.php?n=859 . See footnote 171.

[214]*Deus caritas est*, #28.

[215] Catechism of the Catholic Church, # 2359. Also, "in accepted discipline we trade freedom of the ego (freedom to do  or not to do whatever the ego wants) for freedom from the ego (freedom to do what our true nature wants). Here, we ourselves are, as the inner master in our own true nature, the guiding authority;" in "The Call for the Master," by Karl Graf Dürckheim, *PARABOLA,* Spring 1989, page 12.

[216]  In astrophysical terms, "Our universe has no edge or boundary - there is no OUTSIDE of our universe;" www.atlasoftheuniverse.com/bigbang.html .

217 "Love is "divine" because it comes from God and unites us to God; through this unifying process it makes us a "we" which transcends our divisions and makes us one, until in the end God is "all in all" (*1 Cor* 15:28)", *Deua Caritas Est,*. Part I, # 18. Illustration: Michelangelo, "The Last Judgment," Sistine Chapel, Vatican.

218 Jesus condemned adultery (*Matthew* 19; 9), lust (adultery in one's heart, *John* 4:16-18), promiscuity (*John* 8:1-11; not written by John). "...a case can be made that Jesus was totally silent on matters relating to sexual behavior except for the special case involving obsessive feelings of lust towards a married person other than one's spouse;" B.A. Robinson, "Human sexuality What did Jesus' say about sex?", Ontario Consultants on Religious Tolerance. 07-2007.

219 Benedict XVI, Love is the Only Force That Can Truly Transform the World. Mass at Bresso Park in Milan, Italy, 3 June, 2012 (VIS).

220 God's plan "includes all the men and women of the world, because the call is universal. God excludes no one, His plan is exclusively a plan of love. ..." Benedict XVI, Vatican City, general audience 20 June 2012 (VIS).

221 See Appendix 2, Excerpts from "'Ulysses': A Monologue," in *The Spirit in Man, Art, and Literature,* by C. G. Jung, Princeton University Press, 4th, 1978, pages 109-134.

222 As the 9th century Gregorian hymn assures us, "*Ubi caritas et amor Deus ibi est*"; where love and charity [exist], God is there.

223 'The Holy Spirit will come upon you, and the power of the Most High will cover you with its shadow;" *Luke,* 1; 36.

224 *John* 1; 14.

225 See "The Jewish Roots of Family Values" by Don Feder in www.donfeder.com.

226 Numa Denis Fustel de Coulanges, *The Ancient City*, Doubleday Anchor Books, N.Y. 1967.

227 Fustel de Coulanges, *op. cit.,* page 66; *Genesis*, 12 ; 7.

[228] R. T. France, *The Gospel of Matthew*.
hegospelcoalition.org/blogs/justintaylor/2011/08/17/7-differences-between-galilee-and-judea-in-the-time-of-jesus/
[229] The Jewish Marriage Ceremony "According to the Laws of Moses and Israel": by Maurice Lamm,
http://www.chabad.org/library/article_cdo/aid/465162/jewish/The-Jewish-Marriage-Ceremony.htm
[230] St. Augustine, *op. cit.* # 6: "*Oportebat enim caput nostrum propter insigne miraculum secundum carne nasci de virgine, quo significaret membra sua de virgine Ecclesia scundum spiritum nascitura. Sola ergo Maria et spiritu [Ecclesiae] et corpore [Christi] mater et virgo…*"
[231] Specifically, *Genesis,* 9; 1, 7, 22. *Genesis* 12; 1-25 (Abraham, father of nations).
[232] "When a family becomes extinct, a worship dies out […] In view of these opinions, celibacy was a grave impiety and a misfortune…" *The Ancient City,* page 50. Jesus triumphed over death: his resurrection assured not the continuity of the old religion but its fulfillment and the establishment of the New Law of Love.
[233] St. Augustine, *op. cit* # 4.
[234] *Proverbs*, 9; 10 and *Psalm* 111, 10.
[235] See Appendix "On Revolution".
[236] *Genesis*, 1 and 2.
[237] *The Ancient City,* page 392.
[238] *Galatians* 3:28.
[239] "This greeting [the Annunciation] announces the end of the sadness of the world in relation to the limits of life, suffering…the darkness of the evil that seems to obscure the light of divine goodness. It is a greeting that marks the beginning of the Gospel;" Benedict XVI, General Audience, December 19, 2012, Vatican City.
[240] Benedict XVI, *Deus.caritas.est,* Part I, # 8.
[241] Benedict XVI: "It is rational to believe," Vatican City, Wednesday, general audience, 21 November 2012.
[242] *Deus caritas est*, Part I, 11.

[243] "Through him all things came to be, not one thing had its being but through him;" *John*, 1; 3.

[244] Benedict XVI, general audience, 21 November 2012.

[245] "…the command of love of neighbor is inscribed by the Creator in man's very nature." *Deus caritas est*, Part II, # 31.

[246] "I am not in hell, and yet you are there too, for *if I sink down to the world beneath, you are present still*;" Saint Augustine quotes Psalm 138:8 in *Confessions*, Book I, Chapter 2.

[247] *John*, 1; 1.

[248] St. Irenaeus, writing around 180 A.D., "The Word of God, our Lord Jesus Christ, who did, through His transcendent love, become what we are, that He might bring us to be even what He is Himself." Also, "…He was God, and then became man, and that to deify us," Athanasius, c 350 A.D.

[249] "He came to his own domain and his own people did not accept him. But to all who did accept him he gave power to become children of God, to all who believe in his name who was born not out of human stock or urge of the flesh or will of man but of God himself. The Word was made flesh;" *John*, 1; 11-14.

[250] C. S. Lewis, *Miracles*, opening sentence, Chapter 2, page 5.

[251] Lewis, *op.cit.*, Chapter 8, page 60.

[252] The formulation made by Teilhard de Chardin distinguishing a materialist and a spiritualist world view, quoted by then professor Joseph Ratzinger in a radio talk delivered in 1968; see *Creation and Evolution*, pages 13-14.

[253] Theology professor Joseph Ratzinger, radio broadcast, 1968; quoted by Christoph Cardinal Schönborn in *Creation and Evolution, a Conference with Pope Benedict XVI*, 2008, page 14; emphasis added.

[254] "Gospel stories, myths and legends," January 2, 2013 By Fr. Dwight Longenecker in http://www.patheos.com/blogs/standingonmyhead/2013/01/gospel-stories-myths-and-legends.html.

[255] Longenecker, *loc.cit*

[256] *Deus Caritas Est*, 1, 18.

[257] *Matthew*, 1; 23.

[258] "The Christian picture of the world is this, that the world in its details is the product of a long process of evolution but that at the most profound level it comes from the *Logos*. Thus it carries rationality within itself;" Benedict XVI, *Truth and Tolerance: Christian Belief and World Religions*, quoted in *Creation and Evolution,* page 22.

[259] G. K. Chesterton, *St. Thomas Aquinas*, Image Books, N.Y., 1955, page 37.

[260] Thomas Merton, *Love and Living*, Bantam Books, N.Y., 1981, page104.

[261] Most materialist thinkers still consider the biological reproduction "the primary end of the family [is] the procreation of children."

[262] *John* 14, 6, **John 1:4, John 11:25,** *1 John,* 5; 20, respectively.

[263] *Catechism*, pages 560-576.

[264] *Ibid.* page 567: the passage of Pope John Paul II is from his encyclical *Familiaris Consortio*, # 11.

[265] *Gaudium et Spes,* # 50, 2, pastoral constitution, Pope Paul VI, 12-07-1965.

[266] *John* 13; 34-35.

[267] *Galatians* 3, 28.

[268] "Faith means knowing God as Love, thanks to His own love. The love of God … opens our eyes and allows us to know all reality beyond the limited horizons of individualism and subjectivism which distort our awareness". Benedict XVI: "It Is Rational To Believe," Vatican City, 21 November 2012. See also Farley, *Just Love*, page 290 in which she treats the subject of "Fruitfulness."

[269] See Part I, Chapter 3: "One generation's sexual revolution."

[270] St. Augustine, *Confessions,* VIII, 7.

[271] *Confessions*, loc. cit.

[272] Hannah Arendt, *Love and Saint Augustine*, University of Chicago Press, 1996, pages 9-44.

[273] Arendt, loc. cit. pages 18-19.

[274] Ibid. page 19.

[275] *Confessions*, I,1.

[276] *De Motu ad Magistrum Philipum,* published in 1273.

[277] Aquinas, *De Motu Cordis*, #456: *"Similiter ex parte appetitus appetere ultimum finem, qui est felicitas, est homini naturale, et fugere miseriam; sed appetere alia non est ei naturale, sed ex appetitu ultimi finis procedit in appetitu aliorum: sic est enim finis in appetibilibus,… Sic ergo cum motus omnium aliorum membrorum ex motu cordis causetur…motus quidem alii possunt esse voluntarii, sed primus motus qui est cordis, est naturalis."*

[278] Pope Pius XII, October 29, 1951. See footnotes 199-200, page 95 above: *Qur'an* Sûras 4 # 34 and 66 # 1 respectively.

[279] Fuchs, op. cit., page 142. I learned that Fr. Fuchs was Pope Pius XII's spiritual director while studying theology at the Gregorian University in Rome.

[280] Ibid. page 152.

[281] *De Motu Cordis, # 454: "unde et homo qui est perfectissimus animalium, dicitur a quibusdam minor mundus."*

[282] From "Making sense out of suffering", by Peter Kreeft, in Eric Metaxas, *Socrates in the city,* Dutton, 2011, page 59.

[283] *Luke,* 1:46-55.

[284] *Catechism*, Numerals 164-165: "the Blessed Virgin advanced in her pilgrimage of faith, and faithfully persevered in her union with her Son unto the cross, where she stood, in keeping with the divine plan,(294) grieving exceedingly with her only begotten Son, uniting herself with a maternal heart with His sacrifice, and lovingly consenting to the immolation of this Victim which she herself had brought forth. Finally, she was given by the same Christ Jesus dying on the cross as a mother to His disciple with these words: "Woman, behold thy son;" Pope Paul VI, November 21, 1964, *Lumen Gentium #58* and, "At the foot of the Cross Mary shares through faith in the

shocking mystery of this self- emptying. This is perhaps the deepest "kenosis" of faith in human history. Through faith the Mother shares in the death of her Son, in his redeeming death; but in contrast with the faith of the disciples who fled, hers was far more enlightened. On Golgotha, Jesus through the Cross definitively confirmed that he was the "sign of contra-diction" foretold by Simeon," in Pope John Paul II, *The Mother of the Redeemer*, March 25, the Solemnity of the Annunciation of the Lord, in the year 1987. Regarding "shaking" our faith, see *John*, 16; 1: "'I have told you all this so that *your faith may not be shaken'*".

[285] " ... when this mortal nature has put on immortality, then the words of scripture will come true: *Death is swallowed up in victory. 'Death, where is your victory? Death, where is your sting?'* Now the sting of death is sin, and sin gets its power from the Law. So let us thank God for giving us the victory through our Lord Jesus Christ;" *1 Corinthians*, 15; 34-37.

[286] *John*, 10; 17: "The Father loves me, because I lay down my life in order too take it up again, No one takes it from me; I lay it down of my own free will..."

[287] *Luke*, 23; 42, 43: "'Jesus,' he said, 'remember me when you come into your kingdom.' 'Indeed, I promise you,' he replied, 'today you will be with me in paradise."

[288] *Genesis* 17.

[289] See *Mark*, 14; 22-24.

[290] See "Answering an Atheist and Asking for Fairness and Accuracy" by: Msgr. Charles Pope, in
http://blog.adw.org/2013/01/answering-an-atheist-and-asking-for-fairness-and-accuracy/ .

291 As was mentioned above, throughout history we find thinkers, theologians, religious and civil leaders making futile attempts at defining and "resolving" the problem of human death and suffering. Kreeft's lecture (Note 292) contains a sentence which attests to the nature of both human suffering and death: "Hush, child, you couldn't possibly understand. Who do you think you are, anyway? *I am* the Author; you are the character." In other words, we are dealing with our transcendent Author, the Mystery. C.S. Lewis' *The Problem of Pain* is an excellent analysis from a Christian perspective.

292 Although it refers to a specific sacrament, Numeral 1521 of the *Catechism* addresses the problem of suffering and death: "By the grace of this sacrament (Anointing of the sick) the sick person receives the strength and the gift of uniting himself more closely to Christ's Passion: in a certain way he is *consecrated* to bear fruit by configuration to the Savior's redemptive Passion. **Suffering**, a consequence of original sin, **acquires a new meaning: it becomes a participation in the saving work of Jesus;**" (emphasis added). Needless to say the "new meaning" results from the New Law of Love.

293 "The only thing we can do about suffering is to live through it," Metaxas, op. cit., page 48.

294 See Part I chapter 3: My Generation's Sexual Revolution, page 16 above.

295 "Today we celebrate the Feast of the Baptism of Jesus: the Child, the son of the Virgin, whom we contemplated in the mystery of his birth, we see today an adult emerging himself in the waters of the Jordan River, thus sanctifying the waters and the entire cosmos." Pope Benedict: "May we be renewed in our Baptism, January 13, 2013, Vatican Radio.

296 Benedict XVI, *Deus Caritas Est, I, # 5.*

297 Hannah Arendt, *On Revolution,* Penguin Books, 1990; chapter 1, "The Meaning of Revolution."

# BIBLIOGRAPHY

The titles cited in this book are indicated in the text. The additional bibliographical information given below in alphabetical order refers to works that complement or illustrate the reading.

Aeschylus, *Agamemnon: Four Famous Greek Plays.* Edited with an introduction by Paul Landis, Modern Library, N.Y., 1929.

Anselm, St. *Monologium,* in *Basic Writings.* Translated by S. N. Deane with an introduction by Charles Harshorne, 2nd. Open Court, La Salle, 1974.

Aquinas, Thomas St. *Summa Theologica,* II-IIae, 53, 1. *Summa Theologica,* III, 68, 11."De Potentia Dei" and "De Motu Cordis," *Opuscula Philosophica.* Marietti, Milan, 1954.

Arendt, Hannah, *Love and Saint Augustine*, University of Chicago Press, 1996. *On Revolution*, Penguin Books, 1977. *The Life of the Mind*, Harcourt Brace & Co., 1977.

Aristotle, *On the Soul*: in *The Basic Works of Aristotle.* Edited and with an Introduction by Richard McKeon, Random House. N.Y. 1941. *Protrepticus*, A Reconstruction, Anton-Hermann Chroust, University of Notre Dame Press, 1964.

Augustine, St. *Confessions.* Translated with an Introduction by R. S. Pine-Coffin. Penguin Books, London 1961. H*omily on 1 St. John's Epistle; On Saint John's Gospel; On Sacred Virginity; The City of God.*

Barron, Mons. Robert Herman Lecture 2012. Just Quietly Productions, 2012.

Barton, Bruce, *What can a man believe?* Bobbs Merrill Co., Indianapolis, 1927.

Benedict XVI, Pope, *Caritas in Veritate*, Encyclical: Libreria Editrice Vaticana, 2009. *Deus Caritas Est*, Encyclical: Libreria Editrice Vaticana, 2005. *Homilies(by dates ; source, Vatican Information Service):* 04-29-2012 ;    05-27-2012 ;    06-03-2012, "Love is the only force that can truly…" 06-20-2012, "On God's plan"; 10-04-2012 (Loreto); 11-21, 2012, "It is rational to believe."11-24-2012; 12-19-2012; 12-08-2012, "The Power if Grace…"; *Creation and Evolution, A Conference with Pope Benedict XVI in Castel Gandolfo*, Tr. Michael J. Miller, Ignatius Press, 2008.

Boccaccio, Giovanni. *Decameron.*

Boudiba, A.    *La Sexualidad en el Islam.*  Caracas, 1980.

Brill, A. A. "The savage's dread of incest." http://archive.org/details/totem_and_taboo_1007_librivox.

Campbell, Joseph.    *Mythic Worlds, Modern Words, on the art of James Joyce.* Edited by Edmund L. Epstein, Harper-Collins, N.Y., 1993.

Carroll, William. "Thomas Aquinas and Big Bang Cosmology." http://maritain.nd.edu/jmc

*Catechism of the Catholic Church.*  Libreria Editrice Vaticana, 1994.

Chesterton, G. K. *St. Thomas Aquinas.* Image Book, N.Y., 1956. *The Everlasting Man.* Dover Publications, N.Y., 2007.

Comte-Sponville, André. *The Little Book of Atheist Spirituality.* Translated by Nancy Huston, Viking, N.Y., 2007.

*Creation and Evolution, A Conference with Pope Benedict XVI in Castel Gandolfo.* Translated by Michael J. Miller. Ignatius Press, 2008.

Dante. *Divine Comedy,* Paradise, # 33.

Darwin, Charles. *On the Origin of the Species.*

Dawkins, Richard. *The God Delusion,* Houghton Mifflin Co., N.Y., 2006.

De Chardin, Pierre Teilhard, S.J. *The Phenomenon of Man.* Introduction by Sir Julian Huxley. Harper Colophon Books. N.Y., 1961.

De Coulanges. see Fustel de Coulanges.

De Rougemont, Denis. *Love in the Western World.* Harper Torchbooks, N.Y., 1956.

Derrida, Jacques. *The Gift of Death.* University of Chicago Press, 1992.

Dickens, Charles. *Tale of Two Cities* (chapter 1).

Donne, John. *Devotions upon emergent occasions, Meditation.*

Dostoyevsky, Fyodor. *The Brothers Karamazov.*

Eliot, T. S. "The Rock" (poem) in *The Waste Land and other poems*, Harvest Book. San Diego, 1958.

Farley, Dr. Margaret A. *Just Love, a framework for Christian Ethics.* Continuum. N.Y., 2006.

Feder, Don. "The Jewish roots of family values," www.donfeder.com.

France, R. T. "The Gospel of Matthew," http://thegospelcoalition.org/blogs.

Fuchs, Josef, S.J. *Natural Law, A Theological Investiga-Tion.* Translated by Helmut Reckter, S.J. and John A. Dowling. Sheed and Ward, N.Y., 1965.

Fustel deCoulanges, Numa. *The Ancient City.* Doubleday Anchor Book, N.Y.1967.

Graf-Durckhein. "The Call for the Master." *Parabola,* Spring, 1989.

Gregg, Samuel. "Benedict XVI: God's revolutionary." *Crisis Magazine,* April 16, 2012.

Hawkins, Stephen. *The Grand Design.* 2010.

Jaeger, Werner. *Early Christianity and Greek Paideia.* 1961.

John of the Cross, St. *Dark Night of the Soul,* Dover Publications, Inc. N.Y. 2003.

John Paul II, Pope. "Life in the Spirit Based on True Freedom." *L'Osservatore Romano,* 19 January 1981. *"Ut Unum Sint,"* Encyclical. 1995. " *Fides et Ratio,"* Encyclical. 1998.

Jung, C. G. *The Spirit in Man, Art, and Literature.* Translated by R.F.C. Hull, Princeton University Press, 1978.

Kainz, Howard. "Homosexuality, Civil Rights, and Natural Law." www.thecatholicthing.org.

Kierkegaard, Soren. *Purity of Heart is to Will one Thing.* Fontana books, London, 1961.

King, Jr., Dr. Martin Luther. *Letter from a Birmingham Jail.* 1963.

Kreeft, Peter. "Making Sense out of Suffering," in *Socrates in the City, Conversations on "Life, God, and other Small Topics."* Dutton, N.Y., 2011.

Lamm, Maurice. "The Jewish Marriage Ceremony according to the Laws of Moses and Israel." www.chabad.org/library/article.

Lampedusa, G. T. Di. *Il Gattopardo.* Feltrinelli Editore, Milano, 1962.

Latz, Leo J., M.D. *The Rhythm of sterility and fertility in women.* Latz Foundation, Chicago, 14th, 1942.

Lewis, Bernard. *The Middle East: A Brief History of the Last 2,000 Years.* Scribner, N.Y., 2003.

Lewis, C. S. *Mere Christianity.* Macmillan Publishing Co., N.Y., 1960. *Miracles: A preliminary study.* Macmillan Publishing Co., N.Y. 1978. *The Everlasting Man.* Dover Publications, Inc., N.Y. 2007. *The Problem of Pain.* Macmillan Publishing Co., N.Y. 1962. *The Screwtape Letters.* Macmillan Publishing Co., N.Y. 1961. *Miracles: A preliminary study.* Macmillan Paperback, 1978.

Longenecker, Fr. Dwight. *Paganism and Christianity.* http://www.patheos.com/AboutPatheos/

Dwight-Longenecker.html, October 12, 2012.

Machiavelli, N. *The Prince.*

Markel, Howard. *An Anatomy of Addiction: Sigmund Freud, William Halsted, and the Miracle Drug Co-Caine.* Pantheon, N.Y., 2011.

McDowell, Josh. "How did Jesus view the Old Tes-Tament?" in *Reasons Skeptics Should Consider Christianity.* Tyndale House, 1981.

Merton, Thomas. *Love and Living.* Edited by Naomi Burton Stone and Brother Patrick Hart. Bantam Books, 1981.

Metaxas, Eric. *Socrates in the City, Conversations on 'Life, God, and other Small Topics.'* Dutton, N.Y., 2011.

Meyer, Stephen C. *Signature in the Cell, DNA and the Evidence for Intelligent Design.* Harper One, N.Y., 2009.

Mill, John Stuart. *On Utilitarianism.*

Miller, Lisa. "Why is the woman often the victim?" *The Washington Post,* page B-2, November 17, 2012. " Where bishops have trouble under-standing Young Sex" *The Washington Post,* page B-2, February 9, 2013.

Nasr, Vali. *The Shia Revival: how conflict within Islam will shape the future.* W.W. Norton & Co., N.Y., 2006.

Needleman, Jacob. "The Great Unknown is Me, Myself." *Parabola.* Fall, 2012.

Novak, Michael. *The Experience of Nothingness.* Harper Colophon Books, N.Y., 1971.

Ortega y Gasset, José. *Estudios sobre el Amor*, Revista
de Occidente. Madrid, 1964. *Meditaciones del Quijote*, Revista de Occidente, Madrid, 1963.

Paul VI, Pope. *Gaudium et Spes,* 1965.

Pius IX, Pope. *Ineffabilis Deus,* 1854.

Pius XII, Pope. *Allocution to Midwives,,* October 29,
1951.

Plato. *Symposium, Theaetetus, and Ion*, in *The Collected
Works of Plato, including the Letters*, edited by Edith
Hamilton and Huntington Cairns, Bollingen Series,
Pantheon Books, N.Y., 1961.

Rand, Ayn. *The Virtue of Selfishness: A New Concept
of Egoism.* The New American Library, 5th, 1964.

Ridgway, Ian. "Freud and Humanist Judaism."
http://www.myauz.com/ianr/articles/lect4
freud%20&hHumanistjudaism07.pdf

Robinson, B. A. "Human Sexuality: what did Jesus
say about sex?" http://www.salon.com/ 2012/09
/16/ gene_robinson_conservatives_should_ sup-
port_gay_marriage/

Sayers, Dorothy L. *The Mind of the Maker.* Living
Age Books, N.Y., 1956.

Shakespeare, Wm.    *Hamlet* and *Romeo and Juliet.*

Singer, Isaac Bashevis. *A Young Man in Search of
Love.* Doubleday and Co., N.Y., 1978.

Sinha, Indra. *Kama Sutra.* article in Wikipedia.

Smith, Adam. *The Wealth of Nations.* 1776.

Tennyson, Alfred Lord. *The Princess*, a poem.

Teilhard de Chardin  see de Chardin.

*The Emperor Jones.* John Krimsky & Gifford Cochran, 1933 film version of Eugene O'Neill's play by the same name.

Tillich, Paul. *The Courage to Be.* Yale University Press,1952. *The Eternal Now.* Charles Scribner's Sons, N.Y., 1963.

Urwin, John.   "One of the Many Quirks of Quantum: Perpetual Motion and Never-ending Currents." *Yale Scientific*, April 2012.

Vatican Council II.     *Message to Humanity*, October 20, 1962. *The Documents of Vatican II.*  Guild Press, N.Y., 1966.

Wellman, Robert R.     "Socrates and Alcibiades — the Major," www.blissofpeace.com.

Wolf, Naomi. "Kate's breasts, Pussy Riot, Virginity Tests, and Our Attitudes on Women's Bodies." CNN, 07/19/2012.

Wordsworth, William. *My Heart Leaps Up* (poem).

Wilde, Oscar. *Ave Maria Plena Gratia.* In *The Works of Oscar Wilde including the poems, novels, plays, essays, fairy tales, and dialogues.* Black's Readers Service Co., N. Y., 1927.

Xavier S.J.  St. Francis Letter to Saint Ignatius of Loyola, 1543. http://www.fordham.edu/halsall/mod/1543xavier1.asp

18335104R00115

Made in the USA
Charleston, SC
28 March 2013